Aid Performance and Development Policies of Western Countries

Overseas Development Institute,

edited by
Bruce Dinwiddy

Published in association with the
Overseas Development Institute

Aid Performance and Development Policies of Western Countries

Studies in US, UK, E.E.C., and Dutch Programs

Praeger Publishers   New York   Washington   London

PRAEGER PUBLISHERS
111 Fourth Avenue, New York, N.Y. 10003, U.S.A.
5, Cromwell Place, London S.W.7, England

Published in the United States of America in 1973
by Praeger Publishers, Inc.

Library of Congress Catalog Card Number: 72-93188

Printed in the United States of America

Contents

List of Tables

Appendixes

Aid Performance and Development Policies of Western Countries

Introduction

A recent survey has shown that there is wide public support, particularly among the relatively well educated and informed, for the principle of British assistance to the development of poorer countries[1]. There continues to be discussion concerning the best *means* of assisting development; and this debate, in other rich countries as well as Britain, has been an important factor in the emergence of a broader understanding of developing countries' problems, coupled with a greater awareness that the interests of developing countries are vitally affected by rich country decisions on a wide range of domestic and international issues. A rich country's development assistance policy cannot be isolated from its foreign and economic policies generally.

It has also become increasingly appreciated that 'development' is a much longer and more complicated process than used sometimes to be thought; and this, too, has served to move the 'aid' debate to a more fundamental level. Proponents of an improved development assistance effort have previously tended to concentrate on the need of, for example, a *larger* aid programme. The need is there. As will be seen in Chapter 1, the volume of international official aid is remarkably small; and it has been diminishing. But pressure for a larger aid effort is no substitute for continuous and critical appraisal of what aid is doing. Increased attention has therefore been focused on the developing countries themselves; and in this context two distinct lines of current thinking may be identified.

First, there has been a shift in the intellectual approach to development. Although the most widely publicised target of the First Development Decade – an average economic growth-rate in developing countries of 5% per annum – was achieved, many of the benefits have been confined to relatively small numbers of people; and ironically, the most immediate effects of such wider social improvements as have been achieved, notably in health and education, have been to increase the challenge of development, by accelerating the rate of population growth and substantially increasing the numbers in search of jobs. These shortcomings have been recognised in the UN strategy for the Second Development Decade[2] :

[1] See I. Rauta, *Aid and Overseas Development*, HMSO, 1971.
[2] *International Development Strategy*, UN, New York, 1970, para 18.

3

'As the ultimate purpose of development is to provide increasing opportunities to all people for a better life, it is essential to bring about a more equitable distribution of income and wealth for promoting both social justice and efficiency of production, to raise substantially the level of employment, to achieve a greater degree of income security, to expand and improve facilities for education, health, nutrition, housing and social welfare, and to safeguard the environment.'

The UN strategy for the 1970s thus also recognises the second new line of thinking which has been emerging in the last few years : concerning possible implications of 'development' for the human environment. At present, as Guy Hunter points out in Chapter 7, the main responsibility for the environmental threat lies with the rich rather than the poor world. Pollution arises largely from the activities of industrialised countries (although its effects are already spreading much more widely) and it is also these countries which are placing the heaviest, and most rapidly increasing, demands on the world's non-renewable resources. Sooner or later, rich countries will be forced to cut back on this growth of consumption, and they will almost certainly have to adopt more active policies of population control. Equally, it must be recognised that any threat to the quality of the global environment that is presented by mere numbers of people comes mainly from the developing countries, who may, according to current projections, eventually account for between 85% and 90% of the world's total population[1].

In his latest Review[2], Edwin Martin, Chairman of OECD's Development Assistance Committee (DAC), observes that there is the possibility of reconciling the problems of rapidly expanding production in rich countries and population growth in poor countries. As he points out, a slowing of growth in industrialised countries would imply a slackening in demand for exports from developing countries, and would in itself also tend to restrict the growth prospects of the latter. A sensible course for industrialised countries to adopt, therefore, would be to cut back production for their own consumption and to take special measures to transfer resources to the poor countries. This would conform with social justice; but in addition, the resultant improvement in the quality of the lives of people in developing countries 'could help greatly to produce the parental motivation necessary to bring their rate of population growth down to the levels required for man to

[1]See Robert S. McNamara, *Address to the Board of Governors of the World Bank*, September 1971.
[2]*Development Assistance*, 1971 Review, OECD (hereinafter referred to as *DAC Review*).

survive comfortably over the long-term'. This proposal deserves detailed consideration; and an important step towards its implementation could be taken through linking international development assistance to the creation of Special Drawing Rights (SDRs)[1].

As we advance into the Second Development Decade, an important lesson can be drawn from the experience of the 1960s. There can no longer be any pretence that there is one 'right' direction for development – neither for the developing world as a whole, nor even for any particular developing country. It is for this reason that, although this Review contains many references to the importance of ensuring that external assistance is directed to promoting development, no attempt can be made to define – except in the most abstract terms – what 'development' involves. Each developing country is confronted with different problems and possibilities; and attempts to graft alien patterns on to its own cultural base (as, for example, by too closely copying Western education systems, or allowing the economy to become dominated by large-scale foreign investment) may lead to social discord and eventual rejection. It follows that rich countries should not allow their approach to development assistance to be irrelevantly prejudiced by their own cultural background and attitudes.

On the other hand, a completely passive assistance policy is neither practicable nor desirable. Each donor must decide where its aid should go (even if it provides most of its aid multilaterally, it still has to compare different international organisations in order to choose between them) : moreover, if aid is given for humanitarian purposes, the donor must form some opinion as to whether the recipient regime's strategy is likely to promote them. Not all governments in developing countries are equally motivated by a desire to improve the lot of their people.

The developing countries' demands for a voice in discussions on world monetary reform have so far (as is noted in Chapter 1) met with little success. Developing countries still have very little influence in GATT; and even where rich countries make voluntary concessions, as many of them have recently done, for example, by introducing General Preference schemes for the imports of manufactures from developing countries, these exclude some of the items in which developing countries are gaining, or have gained, a comparative advantage (thus textiles are excluded from most donors' offers)[2]. Moreover, different developing countries and regions naturally have different interests and priorities : most tropical African countries at present have virtually nothing to gain from the new preference schemes. It is therefore not surprising that the 'Group of 77' (now composed of some 95 countries) finds it so difficult to adopt a common line in negotiations

[1]See page 12.
[2]See Chapters 1, 3 and 6, and Appendix B.

5

with the rich world, nor that the agenda for the third UNCTAD conference, in Santiago (April-May 1972), covers such a wide field. With rich countries continuing to be preoccupied with their own short-term economic interests, it would be rashly optimistic to hope for any major breakthroughs at UNCTAD III. But if the conference does degenerate into little more than a slanging-match, it will not be enough merely to ascribe this to the disordered strategy of the poor; the short-sighted selfishness of the rich will also be partly responsible.

The present state of world development assistance, to which most of this Review is devoted, presents a gloomy picture. In Part I, ODI staff examine and comment on British aid performance and development policy, in the context of recent world events and trends. Chapter 1 contains sections on the international monetary situation, the new General Preference schemes, and trade and private investment flows, together with a comparison of the aid performance of all the main Western donors. Despite substantially increased contributions from some countries[1], official development assistance flows declined during the 1960s from 0.52% to 0.34% of the combined GNP of all donors. In recent years it has also fallen in absolute terms. Britain's individual decline, from 0.59% to 0.37%, has been slightly less than that of the United States, but otherwise rather worse than average. The latest public expenditure projections do allow for a moderate expansion of the British aid programme. But this falls far short of the UN 0.7% target[2] – the need for whose existence the Government is not even prepared to recognise. Other aspects of current British development policy – particularly the Government's attitude towards the role of private overseas investment – also receive critical comment.

In Part II, for the first time in an ODI Review, the chapters appear under their authors' names. First, in order to broaden the Review's treatment of the international development assistance effort, there are two chapters, commissioned by ODI from independent authorities in the countries concerned, on the aid and development policies of the United States and the Netherlands.

The chapter on the United States, written by James Howe and Robert Hunter, of the Overseas Development Council, is particularly interesting in view of the recent world economic crisis, precipitated by the introduction of President Nixon's New Economic Policy, and of the Senate defeat of the President's foreign aid bill. It seems that any prospect of an early reversal of the falling trend in US aid would

[1]Notably Australia, Canada, Denmark, the Netherlands and Sweden.
[2]0.7% of donor GNP by 1975.

depend on the recovery of the US economy and, even more important, on renewed political support, based on less ambitious expectations of a quick pay-off, in Washington.

Chapter 5, on the Netherlands, was written (at commendably short notice) by Dick van Geet, of the University of Amsterdam. The Dutch official aid programme has recently been rapidly increased; the Netherlands is one of the five countries which have accepted the 0.7% target; and its development policy – in marked contrast to the US, which cannot escape the political implications of its special position as the world's richest nation and (still) the largest individual aid donor – is less affected by other aspects of foreign policy. More than 20% of Dutch aid is given multilaterally; but it should be noted that most bilateral aid is still effectively tied to the purchase of Dutch goods, and also that relatively large amounts of aid are still devoted to the remaining Dutch dependencies[1]. Perhaps the most interesting theme of the chapter is its discerning analysis of the ways in which a government's development assistance programme can depart – through no fault of the aid administrators themselves – from the precepts of its official aid philosophy.

The last two chapters have been contributed by ODI staff. In Chapter 6, Peter Tulloch provides the background to some of the more worrying aspects, as they affect developing countries, of British entry into the European Economic Community. Compared to Britain, which will have to adapt its policies to those of the Community, the EEC gives greater protection, both to its own farmers and to its own manufacturers, against developing countries' exports. In general, most EEC policies towards developing countries have evolved on an 'ad hoc' basis : the system of association is particularly arbitrary in its discrimination between different countries, and it is suggested that the EEC should reconsider its implicit attitude that there exists any particular geographical and economic 'region' of the developing world with which a European Community of ten members can sensibly identify itself.

Finally, Guy Hunter reminds us that, in view of current rates of world population growth, we are involved in a race against time. He rightly concentrates on the need for recognition that developing countries must find and pursue a course of development which reflects their own capacities and style : the new strategy can still benefit from suitably directed international support, but the major effort must come from within the developing countries themselves.

Bruce Dinwiddy
February 1972

[1] 1971 budgeted disbursements to the Netherlands Antilles and Surinam, whose combined population is barely 600,000, were $58m.

7

PART I

1 International Development Policies

The New American Economic Policy and the International Monetary Situation

The dominant economic event of the past eighteen months has undoubtedly been the unveiling of President Nixon's New Economic Policy (NEP). The primary objective of the NEP is to restore the health of the American economy. But, given its size and importance, major domestic changes inevitably affect other countries, not least the poorer members of the international community, which depend on the US for some 40% of their aid, 30% of their private capital inflows, and 20% of their export markets.

The most important measure has been the decision to devalue the US Dollar, both in terms of gold (7.8%) and a number of leading national currencies – such as the Pound, Mark and Yen. The devaluation of the dollar has been effected within a general agreement on realignment of hard currencies. The new pattern of exchange rates has altered the relative competitiveness of developing countries, as well as the value of their foreign assets and obligations; it has also affected the mechanics of several commodity schemes. As a result they too have had to review the appropriateness of their existing exchange rates, and determine the best course to follow, which, given the uncertain new conditions, has not been easy.

The realignment of exchange rates, while it is an important step towards restoring external equilibrium for the US, does not guarantee that this will be achieved. Certainly, it will be difficult to maintain equilibrium for any length of time unless further adjustments are made in the present international monetary system. The American deficit has been an important element in the functioning of the system as it has developed since the 1950s; it provided the main source of new international liquidity needed to finance trade expansion and the accumulation of large payments surpluses by Japan and several European countries at a time of slowly expanding stocks of monetary gold. The removal of the US deficit thus requires some alternative injection of liquidity.

The US is anxious to see an enhanced role for 'paper gold', which in time would largely displace both gold and national currencies for international reserve purposes. A substantial expansion in new Special Drawing Rights (SDRs) – or some similar substitute – seems to be

8

envisaged. This would be a positive step, which Britain also favours[1], but which meets with less enthusiasm from the more cautious European Central Banks.

Developing countries share a common interest with developed countries in a solution that would ensure the orderly functioning of the international economy. However, while for developed countries the interest in reform is focused mainly on improvements in the present system, which implies at least a tacit acceptance of the present balance of economic power, developing countries are anxious to promote changes in the system which will give them easier access to additional resources. Since the publication of the Stamp Plan in the early 1960s, various schemes have been proposed which aim at meeting the main wishes of both groups by linking the creation of new international liquidity and the provision of more development finance in one overall reform package. In the negotiations leading up to the 1969 agreement on the current SDR scheme, the 'link' received little serious attention, and the distribution of SDRs was finally based on IMF country quotas. Since these were fixed in relation to a country's GNP and share in world trade, the developed countries took the lion's share. Developing countries did not go empty-handed, all the same; their annual allocation of about $800m is considerably higher than, for example, Britain's yearly aid to them, and equivalent to about 15% of their official aid receipts from all DAC countries.

While lack of progress on the 'link' and the *relatively* low SDR allocation to developing countries reflect their weak bargaining position, the present distribution formula for SDRs also reflects the difficulties in the way of any agreement which can satisfy the many divergent interests of the *developed* countries. In the negotiations leading up to the present SDR scheme, many other suggestions for monetary reform were rejected, including the French proposal for a doubling of the gold price, which would have given poor countries much smaller benefits. The SDR formula, with distribution based on IMF quotas, seems to have been chosen largely because it was found acceptable to all countries whose agreement was essential for any reforming initiative to succeed. As long as it was envisaged that SDRs should play only a minor role – they currently account for less than 10% of world reserves – a distribution formula which was based largely on expediency may not have been a high price to pay for an agreement which espoused an important new principle and which, moreover, provided some direct benefit to developing countries.

However, if further reforms following the 1971 currency realignment are to include a more extensive use of SDRs, as the Americans envisage, there is a strong case for reviewing the IMF quota-based distribu-

[1]See, for example, the speech by the Chancellor of the Exchequer before the 1971 IBRD/IMF Annual General Meeting.

tion. Ordinary IMF quotas entail both privileges and obligations; they are based on the simple principle that the more a country contributes, the more it can borrow when in need. But there is no corresponding obligation in the case of SDRs; they are virtually free assets for their recipients. If SDRs are to be created at an accelerating rate, it should become increasingly difficult – on simple grounds of equity – for the richer countries to justify their taking the bulk for themselves.

At their preparatory conference for UNCTAD III, at Lima, the developing countries decided to set up a small inter-government group to study monetary reform. Their demands for a voice in decisions on monetary reform have so far met with no success. While one sympathises with these countries for the lack of interest in their special problems shown by the Group of Ten or even the IMF, it is as unrealistic to expect that the richer countries would be prepared to see decisions taken within a body such as UNCTAD, as it is to expect that any workable solution could emerge from it. Developing countries could however still play a role in the evolution of the monetary system if the body now to be set up can concentrate on professional examination of possible formulae to link SDRs with development financing. The question of how best to distribute new SDRs is likely to loom large for many years and would not be foreclosed by any bargain, covering the immediate future, struck among the Group of Ten. Nor should past failure to get the 'link' be taken as evidence that it is doomed, since it has already managed to attract some support within governments or Central Banks of developed countries – most notably in Britain, Italy and Sweden.

Evolution of the Multilateral System

Since the inauguration of the First Development Decade in 1961 and, more especially, the founding of UNCTAD in 1964, multilateral institutions have provided the main forum for debate on the many facets of the rich-poor relationship, from trade policy to resource flows through public and private channels. Besides this, they have managed to more than treble their total spending since 1961, so that 10% of all resource flows to developing countries are now channelled through them, compared with less than 5% in the first three years of the decade[1]. The expanded aid budgets have also helped to strengthen their influence on aid-giving practices generally. Three current developments – in the UN Development Programme, the World Bank and the Regional Banks – look like enhancing their influence still further.

As a consequence of the Jackson Report recommendations, the UN assistance effort is undergoing a number of organisational changes.

[1] See Table 1.1.

10

The most interesting of these is the evolution of a system of country programming, which is being introduced gradually and will embrace some 20 recipient countries by the time that UNCTAD reconvenes for the Santiago meeting. Country programming is based on a five-year cycle, with multi-year country aid allocations to facilitate recipient programme planning, following joint recipient-UN consultations on the broad outlines of objectives and priority areas, under the direction of the UNDP Resident Representative. The introduction of programming is accompanied by new spending powers for the Resident Representative in respect of Special Fund-type projects.

The Jackson Report was highly critical of the lack of coherence in UNDP programmes, the competition between Specialised Agencies, and the low overall quality of UN technical assistance. The new procedures should help to improve performance by encouraging a more systematic approach to project selection. Much will depend, however, on the quality of the individual country programmes; and on the role played by the Resident Representative. His ability to exercise real supervision of the programming process and of aid projects will still depend both on his personal standing, and on the rapport he is able to create with the local government; one should certainly not under-estimate the new problems that would arise if Resident Representatives merely rubber-stamped hastily drawn up shopping lists purporting to be coherent country programmes.

If the authority of the Resident Representative is effectively strengthened, this should also clear the way for his greater participation in efforts to co-ordinate technical assistance from bilateral donors.

In the past there have been strong sentiments within the UN system in favour of making it responsible for co-ordinating all aid, including capital aid from bilateral as well as other multilateral donors, with the World Bank – formally an Agency within the UN family – playing a subservient role. This view gained little support in the Bank or indeed elsewhere outside the UN system. The Jackson Report has now endorsed a system of dual responsibility for co-ordination, with the Resident Representative looking after technical assistance and the Bank taking care of capital aid. The Bank is now trying to enhance and extend its own co-ordinating role, for which it has already gained considerable experience through presiding over the India and Pakistan Consortia and a dozen or so country Consultative Groups.

Developments within the Bank suggest that it too is giving greater prominence to the country, rather than the project, approach to aid giving. It has announced its intention to make more systematic use of its country Reports as a basis for discussing development needs and priorities in recipient countries, and to work towards an understanding with these countries on the policies that are appropriate for them to pursue. The Bank has also indicated a willingness to consider programme lending on the basis of agreed recipient policies.

More programme lending, and greater emphasis on an overall country approach – through which better inter-donor co-ordination may be achieved – are in principle desirable and enjoy wide support within bilateral aid agencies, in particular in the US. However, despite the new progressive image of the Bank under Robert McNamara, it has not lost its reputation for inflexibility, even arrogance. If the rather rigid control that the Bank exerts over the projects to which it lends is extended to sectoral or national policies once it moves to programme lending, the new approach may prove to be either ineffective or unacceptable to both recipients and other donors. If this should happen, its efforts at better co-ordination may come to nothing, and the responsibility could then well shift to the new Regional Development Banks.

In the last few years a number of these – in particular those serving Africa, Asia and the Caribbean – have established themselves as new, albeit still small, sources of aid. They were originally modelled on the Inter-American Development Bank (IDB), to provide an alternative source of development funds, administered on criteria most appropriate to their area of operation, and with a strong element of recipient self-monitoring : standing somewhere between the bilateral donors and the monolithic, and rich-country controlled, World Bank Group, they were seen as a device for softening increasingly abrasive aid relations. So far, however, they have come to resemble rather more the World Bank, under the more conservative regime of the past, than the IDB. With their insistence on very strict criteria of financial or commercial viability in project lending and their anxiety to establish their reputation in international financial circles, they have denied themselves an early chance for developing their own style. Their prospects of emerging as real *alternatives* to the World Bank may now depend on future relations between the Bank and its borrowers : these may deteriorate as the Bank tries to extend its influence over borrowers' policies.

General Preferences

The establishment of General Preference schemes (GSPs) applied to some of the developed countries' imports from developing countries, represents one of the few positive achievements to emerge from UNCTAD so far. As a concession of principle, General Preferences move away from the insistence by the rich countries in GATT that all countries should receive equal tariff treatment (the most-favoured-nation principle), towards a recognition that there may be a group of countries which should benefit from special concessions by the developed world. Yet the GSP system in its present form appears shakily founded, and its real value in helping to solve developing countries' trade problems (which are increasingly characterised by non-tariff barriers) is questionable.

Such a scheme, to apply to all imports of manufactures from the developing world, was originally proposed by Dr. Raul Prebisch in his report to the first UNCTAD in 1964. But opposition from the United States meant little action until 1967 when, following a major change in US trading policy, the principle was agreed among OECD member countries. In outline, the proposed scheme was to apply to all industrial manufactures and semi-manufactures imported from all developing countries, and in addition to a limited 'positive list' of processed agricultural products, to be agreed case by case.

Originally, it was envisaged that the seventeen developed countries involved should agree on a mutual scheme to be submitted to the Special Committee on Preferences established by UNCTAD II, to come into action during 1970. In practice the interests of the developed countries have diverged so greatly that separate and markedly differing schemes have been proposed. Of these, the only ones in action by the end of 1971 were those of the European Community, Japan and Norway. A British scheme was introduced on 1 January 1972.

The offers made by the developed countries (detailed in Appendix B) vary considerably in scope, product coverage and depth of tariff reduction. However, they fall into two broad categories which can be characterised, on the one hand, by the British and American proposals and, on the other, by those of the EEC and Japan[1].

The two former schemes offer the developing countries a range of agricultural and manufactured goods on which tariffs will be eliminated or reduced and on which unlimited entry will be allowed unless an escape clause, activated on grounds of 'market disruption', is brought into force. Certain products in which developing countries are already regarded as competitive and where competing domestic industries face problems of adjustment (e.g. textiles in both the UK and the US, footwear in the US) are excluded from the offers altogether.

The two latter schemes are based on systems of tariff quotas for manufactures, above which imports from developing countries will pay the full duty rate. Tariff quotas in the EEC scheme are strictly applied to 'sensitive' commodities – such as most textiles, footwear, and a variety of other goods – where developing countries are likely to be relatively competitive – and held in reserve in the majority of other cases. Imports of 'sensitive' commodities in the base year on which quota levels are calculated (1968) were approximately one-third of all imports from developing countries. An escape clause,

[1] See Chapter 7 for a detailed discussion of the UK and EEC systems.

13

similar to those in the UK and US schemes, is applied to agricultural goods.

It is a moot point which type of arrangement offers more scope to developing countries' exports. The restrictiveness of an 'escape clause' system depends entirely on how it is applied. If used only sparingly, it may offer greater trading opportunities than a scheme in which known tariff quotas are established; but if used in an arbitrary and restrictive fashion, it may be much more harmful to developing countries' interests than a known tariff quota system. One of the dangers of a tariff quota system is that of cut-throat price competition among developing countries themselves to get a reasonable share of the duty-free market – a practice which is hardly likely to promote profitable industrial development in developing countries. What can be said about both types of scheme is that the advantages they offer are rather limited and uncertain.

There can therefore be little satisfaction with the position so far. In the first place, the possibility that the United States may not implement its proposal may soon set at risk the schemes put forward by other developed countries, whose governments all stress that the 'burden' of trade concessions must be equitably 'shared'. Secondly, the separation of 'manufacturing' from agricultural products, and the very limited coverage of the latter in all the schemes, shows up both the pressures from agricultural lobbies in developed countries and the questionable assumption that 'industrialisation' is the road towards economic development. It is to be hoped that the future development of the schemes (which are supposed to be regularly reviewed throughout the ten-year period for which they are initially proposed) will extend concessions more liberally to the processed agricultural sector and thus enlarge the number of developing countries which can benefit. Lastly, the growing volume of non-tariff barriers to trade in recent years has reduced the effectiveness of any system of pure tariff preferences. No such scheme can (by itself) solve satisfactorily the market access problems created by restrictive health and labelling regulations, quantitative restrictions, and domestic industrial and agricultural subsidies.

The Pattern of Trade

During the 1960s, world trade increased in value by nearly 150% (from $128 billion in 1960 to $312 billion in 1970), and in volume by 114%. The volume of trade in manufactures rose most rapidly (by 155%) with that in minerals and fuels rising by 98% and that in agricultural goods by 52%.

The developing countries' share of world trade fell from 21% in 1960 to 18% in 1970, continuing the trend of the 1950s. Nevertheless, it must be noted that the developing countries' export performance during the 1960s was markedly better than in the previous decade, and the difference between developed and developing countries' export growth rates was also less marked. Few of the more pessimistic predictions made at the time of UNCTAD I in 1964 appear to have been borne out. The export earnings of non-oil-producing developing countries grew by 6.0% per annum in the sixties as against 0.8% in the fifties; the terms of trade appear to have been more favourable to developing countries than in the previous decade; and the trade balance of the developing world as a whole, which was virtually in equilibrium in 1969, was in deficit by only $1.7 billion in 1970 – compared to the predicted trade gap, for 1970, of up to $20 billion.

Global figures of course conceal substantial differences between the trading performance of individual countries and regions. Appendix Tables A.5 and A.6 show, respectively, the value of exports by area of origin in 1970 and the network of international trade by geographical region in 1960 and 1968. In an examination of trade figures over the decade, two main points stand out. First, that the importance of the developed market economies as an outlet for developing countries' exports has increased, rather than diminished. Within the overall increase, however, Japan and the EEC increased their importance while the US and British shares declined. Second (although no clear correlation between commodity and country export performance can be made), there has been a marked decline in the developing countries' share of trade in agricultural products, which contrasts strongly with their performance in exports of manufactures.

The fall in the developing countries' share of world exports of agricultural primary products is perhaps the most significant trend of the past decade. Three underlying causes can probably be identified. First, the growth of internal demand in developing countries themselves, which – despite the effects of the Green Revolution – has cut surpluses available for export. Second, the continuing tendency towards substitution of artificial and synthetic products for many natural raw materials, which also threatens to invade the realm of food production. Third, the increasing self-sufficiency of developed countries in farm production, encouraged by a marked increase in the protection of agriculture against imports. The most rapidly growing agricultural export commodities have been those in which developed and developing countries compete – such as fats and oils (where exports of soya bean products have risen most rapidly), coarse grains, sugar, and cotton. In most of these cases, the value of exports from developed countries has grown at a rate substantially faster than that of developing countries' exports. The trend was well illustrated in 1970 when, with an almost unprecedented increase in world export earnings from agricultural goods, the income of developing countries rose

15

by only 12% as against almost 20% in developed countries.

The effects on world markets, both of growing farm protection in developed countries and of the Green Revolution, can be illustrated by the state of world trade in rice. World exports of rice constitute a very small proportion of production (2% in 1970), and the small number of developing countries for whom rice exports are relatively important confronted a world market in which an increasing proportion of exports derived from the surpluses built up by developed countries – principally Japan and Italy – as a result of domestic agricultural incentives. Exports of these surpluses at marginal or subsidised rates have driven down prices. At the same time, increases in output resulting from the introduction of new varieties and improved farming methods have enabled some developing countries which were, in the past, major importers to become largely self-sufficient. Consequently, since 1967 the annual value of world trade in rice has fallen from $1,077m to $922m, and the developing countries' share of the market from 49% to 45%.

Table 1.1   Exports of Manufactures[1] from Developing Countries, 1962 and 1969

Country[2]	1962 Exports	% of LDC Total	1969 Exports	% of LDC Total	% Growth 1962–69
Hong Kong	412	16·4	1,484	23·0	259
Taiwan	65	2·6	570	8·8	782
India	363	14·4	547	8·5	51
Yugoslavia	183	7·3	513	8·0	180
Mexico	107	4·3	379	5·9	255
South Korea	7	0·3	365	5·7	4,535
Brazil	86	3·4	244	3·8	186
Argentina	96	3·8	208	3·2	117
Pakistan	44	1·8	197	3·0	343
Israel	52	2·1	158	2·4	203
Philippines	70	2·8	138	2·1	97
Iran	74	3·0	133	2·1	79
Malaysia	41	1·6	130	2·0	219
Algeria	272	10·8	117	1·8	−57
Ghana	32	1·3	113	1·8	254
Morocco	62	2·5	70	1·1	13
Singapore	12	0·5	70	1·1	462
Ivory Coast	8	0·3	60	0·9	657
Bermuda	6	0·2	52	0·8	757
Cameroon	27	1·1	48	0·7	74
Other LDCs	496	19·7	852	13·2	104
Total	2,515	100·0	6,447	100·0	156

The amounts are in $m.

Notes: 1. 'Manufactures' exclude petroleum products and unworked non-ferrous metals.
   2. Countries are arranged in descending order of magnitude for 1969.
Source: *Trade in Manufactures of Developing Countries, 1970 Review,* UNCTAD, 1971.

In contrast, the share of world exports of manufactures coming from developing countries increased during the decade from 5.5% to 6.6% – a considerable achievement. However, the benefits of the increase remain confined to a relatively small number of countries, mainly in South-East Asia and Latin America (see Table 2.1). In general, high growth rates in exports of manufactures have been achieved by the creation of a highly competitive industrial structure against the background of a favourable governmental attitude to large-scale foreign investment. The first industries in which these developing countries' comparative advantage was shown were those which, broadly, competed with the products of 'old' industries in the developed countries (e.g. clothing and footwear); but more recently rapid growth has taken place in the production of assembled items, with a large labour content, for use as inputs for final production and sale in developed countries (e.g. electronics components).

In the former case, it comes as little surprise that the industries in which developing countries have been broadly successful are some of those in which developed countries are now facing acute problems of adjustment, and which are generally excluded from the new General Preference schemes. By contrast, in the latter case, the financial benefits, in the shape of lower input costs, appear to accrue principally to the industries in developed countries for which the goods are produced; and the net gain to the developing countries is reduced to the extent that profits, royalties and expatriate managerial salaries are remitted abroad. It is questionable, therefore, how much a developing country really benefits from the presence of such industries, over and above the value of local wage payments and the development of some skills – which in themselves may be a considerable economic and social gain.

The Flow of Financial Resources

Resource flows remain difficult to measure with accuracy, despite recent improvements in published information.

The least reliable figures are those for private flows and for aid from communist countries. Both are subject to major revisions, even several years after the year to which they refer, so that statistics on the most recent past are particularly subject to error.

The most comprehensive figures that are available cover official flows from DAC member countries and aid from multilateral organisations; but even these need to be treated with some caution.

In the past, DAC has refrained from committing itself on an actual definition of *aid,* accepting instead all non-military government contributions in cash and kind from member countries made for or on behalf of developing countries (irrespective of their developmental appropriateness or dubious 'aid' character) into a broad category designated as 'the flow of official financial resources'. Since the publication of the Pearson Report this category has been supplemented by a narrower one, termed 'official development assistance', from which official export credits and official loans on non-concessionary (i.e. on commercial) terms have been excluded. This has been a useful step towards the formulation of a precise definition of aid; it should not

17

obscure the fact, however, that the application of the present definition is still unsatisfactory and allows the inclusion of many items which can qualify as development aid on only the most permissive interpretation of that concept. They include, for example, payments made by Britain towards the pensions of former colonial officers who have already left the service of the country in question; they include, also, payments for defence facilities and various related items.

Another problem is the arbitrary line that now separates developing from other countries for purposes of estimating aid flows. There are a number of countries which are relatively well off, but which are included in the developing group – for example Spain and Argentina – and which receive aid which counts in the DAC figures. The 1971 DAC Report contains the suggestion that some of these countries might be 'promoted' out of the developing group. This could help to focus donor attention more clearly on the main problem of poverty and in the longer-run could even lead to a reorientation of help now going to relatively rich countries towards those countries in which the majority of the world's poorest live. There are some twenty countries or territories, with an average annual income of over $700 (eight with incomes over $1,500) now classed as 'developing'. These countries obtained aid commitments in 1967-69 averaging about $300m (grant equivalent) a year. While income should not be taken as the sole, or indeed most important, measure of the level of development, a high income at least indicates a greater possibility of raising development finance from local sources. There is therefore a case for 'promoting' these countries, at least in the sense that aid to them will no longer count towards the UNCTAD and Pearson targets.

Apart from the difficulty of choosing the flows that deserve to qualify as development aid, there are problems of measuring the recorded flows. The global figures which are most commonly quoted and the international targets on which donor performance is assessed – such as the UN targets of 1% of donor GNP for total flows (including aid and private commercial capital) and of 0.7% of GNP for official development assistance alone – are made up of many disparate items. Official development assistance, for example, may be in cash or kind, in free foreign exchange or tied to donor procurement, and may carry restrictive conditions on its use. Its real value may therefore diverge considerably from its nominal value as recorded in aid statistics.

Statistics on resource flows are normally given in 'net' terms. It must be emphasised, however, that in arriving at the net figures, only amortisation and disinvestment are deducted. No allowance is usually made for interest, profit and dividend payments from developing countries to developed countries. The figures therefore overstate the true net resource flow in any given period. The extent of such overstatement will be much greater for private commercial flows (private investment and export credits) than for official development assistance. Both the 1% and 0.7% targets relate to the larger figure, and performance on these targets thus tends to be more flattering to developed countries than it would be on a true net basis. Accordingly, it would seem appropriate to urge DAC members to take steps as soon as possible to measure their performance more realistically.

Table 1.2, which shows the main trends in resource flows reaching developing countries from all quarters (both public and private), should therefore be read in the context of the reservations on reliability and coverage just noted.

The table shows that over the decade as a whole there has been a

Table 1.2 Flow of Resources Reaching Developing Countries, 1961-1970.
(Net of amortisation and disinvestment, current prices)

from	1961–3	1964–6 (annual average)	1967–9	1970 (at 1970 prices)	1970[1] (at 1960 prices)
DAC Countries					
Official development assistance[2]	5,000	5,580	5,665	5,685	4,550
Other official flows	500	210	610	885	785
Private commercial flows	2,675	3,645	5,160	6,390	5,655
Total DAC bilateral flows	8,175	9,445	11,435	12,960[3]	10,990
(as % of overall total)	(92·9)	(88·3)	(90·0)	(88·8)	(..)
Other Industrial Countries					
Total bilateral flows	10	15	15	[20]	[20]
Centrally Planned Economies					
Total bilateral flows	[300]	[395]	[235]	[250]	[..]
(as % of overall total)	(2·2)	(3·7)	(1·9)	(1·6)	(..)
Multilateral Organisations					
Total flows	435	860	1,035	1,500	[1,305]
(as % of overall total)	(4·9)	(8·0)	(8·1)	(9·6)	(..)
Overall Total	8,920	10,715	12,720	14,730[3]	[12,530]

Figures are rounded to nearest $5m. Figures in brackets [] are rough DAC estimates.
.. Not available.

Notes: 1. Based on price index used by OECD (see Sources).
2. In this table, figures for DAC official development assistance include only direct bilateral aid. The figures for multilateral organisations show disbursements, and not the contribution made to them by developed countries. These contributions from DAC countries are shown separately in Table 5, and are included in the total aid figures given in Tables 2 & 3.
3. Excluding voluntary private contributions, amounting to $840m, for which comparable figures for earlier years are not available.

Sources: DAC figures: Development Assistance, 1971 Review, OECD (DAC Review 1971), Tables II-1, Annex II-1.
Other figures: OECD Press Release A(71)22, 28 June 1971, Table 2.

steady, if modest, expansion in the overall flow as estimated by DAC. Between 1961-3 and 1967-9 it increased (at current prices) by some $4,000m, and in 1970 by a further $2,000m. However, taking inflation into account, the real increase between 1961-3 and 1970 was only $3,600m, or some 40%.

Within the overall total, bilateral official development assistance from DAC countries showed a 13% increase in money terms between

1961-3 and 1970, but in real terms there was an actual *decline* by a similar percentage[1].

Bilateral contributions from centrally planned economies have declined, even in money terms. Rather better estimates than in the past are now available for these countries, and they show that their contributions have been considerably smaller than was thought earlier. The new estimates also show a more pronounced peak in the mid-sixties, and a rather rapid decline since then. It should be remembered, however, that these estimates do not record considerable flows to developing communist countries, principally Mongolia, North Korea, North Vietnam, Cuba and Bulgaria, and they therefore underestimate the contribution relative to those recorded for Western sources. However, their inclusion would in all probability not alter the recorded downward trend.

Private flows, in contrast, have risen substantially between 1961-3 and 1970: by $3,700m (or 140%) in money terms, and by $3,000m (or 110%) in real terms. Within this total, there has been a relative decline of portfolio investment as against direct investment, and the share of both has fallen in relation to private export credits. The share of the latter in the private total, which was as low as 20% in the first half of the decade, has in the past few years reached as much as one-third, and is likely to increase still further in the immediate future.

The most striking expansion over the period as a whole has been that of flows from multilateral institutions. Between 1961-3 and 1970, their aid trebled in real terms.

The World Bank Group is continuing to increase its commitment rate at a fast pace; it expects to show a 100% increase in the five-year period 1969-73 compared with the previous five years. Bank disbursements had been relatively stagnant at just under $800m a year since 1967, but in the last financial year (1970/71) they have jumped to $955m. IDA credits have shown a more erratic trend in commitments, reflecting largely the hiatus caused by the slow processes involved in replenishment operations. Fluctuations in disbursements have been rather less pronounced but nevertheless still large. The total for 1970/71 ($235m) was about average in the context of the last half-dozen years.

Negotiations on the third IDA replenishment were completed in August 1970, providing new resources for commitment amounting to just over $800m a year for three years, with effect from July 1971. By that date, however, only ten Part I members had ratified the agreement, a number insufficient to give it effect. Congressional approval was still awaited for the US contribution, which, at $320m a year, is by far the largest. In the meantime, in order to allow IDA to make additional commitments in anticipation of ratification, a number of

[1]Detailed country breakdowns are given in Table 1.3 below.

countries had pledged advanced payments, including Canada ($50m) and Britain ($104m, equivalent to one year's subscription).

In 1970 private voluntary organisations contributed some $840m in grants towards relief work and development projects in the Third World. Figures for earlier years are only tentative, but they nevertheless indicate a rapid upward trend in voluntary aid. In 1970 the largest contribution relative to GNP came from Sweden (0.08%) followed by Canada, Belgium, US and Switzerland (all around 0.06%). The importance of these contributions may be gauged by the fact that in 1970 they were not far short of the World Bank's total lending in the same year.

Official Development Assistance — Performance of DAC Countries

Total official development assistance (net of amortisation) from DAC countries for the last five years is shown below. The record can only be described as dismal.

	$m	% of DAC GNP
1967	6,688	·43
1968	6,400	·38
1969	6,707	·36
1970	6,808	·34
1971 (estimate)	(7,300)	(·35)

The small increase in the DAC total between 1967 and 1970 has been more than offset by higher prices. As a share of the combined GNP of DAC countries, aid has fallen by as much as 20% over the same period. Preliminary figures for 1971 suggest that there has been a reasonable real increase over 1970, and it looks as if the rapid decline in the percentage share in GNP may have been arrested for the first time since the middle of the decade. But the performance falls far short of the 0.7% target for official development assistance.

The idea of a separate target for *official aid* (as a supplement to the UN/UNCTAD 1% target for all flows – comprising both public and private) was first put forward in the Pearson Report, which recommended that 'each aid-giver increase commitments of official development assistance to the level necessary for the net disbursements to reach 0.7% of its GNP by 1975 or shortly thereafter, but in no case later than 1980'[1]. A similar target has since been adopted by the UN as part of the strategy for the Second Development Decade.

Although all DAC countries accepted the UN Development Strategy, only five – Belgium, Denmark, Netherlands, Norway and Sweden – have given an undertaking to meet the Pearson target date. France has undertaken to maintain its aid at between 0.6% and 0.7%

[1]*Partners in Development,* Report of the Commission on International Development ('Pearson Report'), 1969, p.148.

Table 1.3 Outflow of Official Development Assistance (Net¹) to Developing Countries and Multilateral Agencies, 1961-1971

	Cumulative Total		Volume ($m) Annual Average					as a % of GNP Annual Average					Ranking on GNP share Annual Average				
	1961-70	%	1961-3	1964-6	1967-9	1970	[1971]	1961-3	1964-6	1967-9	1970	[1971]	1961-3	1964-6	1967-9	1970	[1971]
Big Five																	
1. US	33,436	54·5	3,267	3,520	3,344	3,050	[3,000]	0·57	0·50	0·38	0·31	[0·29]	3	3	7	11	[11]
2. France	8,711	14·2	923	775	888	951	[1,000]	1·24	0·78	0·70	0·65	[0·67]	1	1	1	1	[2]
3. Germany	4,726	7·7	374	443	559	599	[700]	0·42	0·39	0·41	0·32	[0·36]	6	5=	5=	10	[9]
4. UK	4,520	7·4	431	484	443	447	[490]	0·53	0·49	0·41	0·37	[0·39]	4	4	5=	7=	[8]
5. Japan	2,608	4·2 (88·0)	110	214	392	458	[500]	0·18	0·23	0·28	0·23	[0·22]	8	9=	10=	12	[12]
Middle Six																	
6. Canada	1,485		54	87	206	343	[450]	0·13	0·23	0·31	0·41	[0·47]	11	9=	9	5	[5]
7. Australia	1,280	10·8	80	115	164	203	[220]	0·46	0·51	0·58	0·59	[0·59]	5	2	2	3	[3]
8. Italy	974		70	62	143	147	..	0·16	0·10	0·19	0·16	..	9	14	13	13	[13=]
9. Netherlands	948		53	78	127	196	[250]	0·39	0·36	0·50	0·63	[0·70]	7	7	3	2	[1]
10. Belgium	914		81	83	98	120	[150]	0·62	0·39	0·46	0·48	[0·55]	2	5=	4	4	[4]
11. Sweden	557		17	43	84	117	[180]	0·11	0·21	0·32	0·37	[0·45]	12=	11	8	7=	[6]
Little Four																	
12. Denmark	237		8	15	36	59	[70]	0·11	0·14	0·28	0·38	[0·40]	12=	13	10=	6	[7]
13. Austria	181	1·2	4	25	22	19	..	0·06	0·26	0·15	0·13	..	14=	8	14	15	[15]
14. Norway	168		8	12	24	37	[45]	0·15	0·18	0·26	0·33	[0·35]	10	12	12	9	[10]
15. Switzerland	148		6	11	22	29	..	0·06	0·08	0·13	0·15	..	14=	15	15	14	[13=]
DAC Total	61,281	100·0	5,530	6,029	6,598	6,808	[7,300]	0·54	0·45	0·39	0·34	[0·35]					

.. Not available.   [] Estimate.

Note: 1. Net of amortisation but not of interest.

Source: Based on *DAC Review 1971*, Table II-1, Statistical Table 9, and on information contained in Chapter 2

of its GNP. Two other countries (Germany and Canada) have announced their intention of working towards the 0.7% target, but without committing themselves to a date when this might be reached. Britain, Japan, Australia, Italy, Austria and Switzerland have failed to commit themselves to the 0.7% target; nor do the available projections on aid in these countries suggest that they might reach the target despite the absence of a formal commitment. The US has explicitly rejected the very concept of a target, but has promised to do its best to ensure that its aid will increase.

The record of the individual members (excluding Portugal) for the entire period since DAC was set up is shown in Table 1.3. Most noteworthy, perhaps, is the relatively poor performance, comparing earlier years with later, of the five biggest donors. The particularly disappointing record of the US comes out clearly; it is the only country to register an absolute fall in aid over the decade as a whole.

The most encouraging trend is shown by the middle order donors, four of which have improved their performance on the GNP measure by substantial amounts. By 1971 these countries occupied five out of the top six places in the GNP rankings and accounted for 15% of total aid. Another feature of relative performance is the gradual emergence of a group of countries with medium to small populations as the leaders within DAC. In the early sixties the top six places on the GNP measure were occupied by three big, and three medium-to-small countries; by the end of the decade France alone among the big countries managed to retain its place in that leading group.

For 1969 and 1970 it is now possible to show the relative performance of DAC members either according to disbursements net of all reverse payments, or according to commitments calculated in terms of their grant equivalent. The former is useful as a more accurate indicator of the actual net transfer of aid resources that has taken place in a given period′, while the latter gives a better summary of the real value of current aid intentions. Relative performances for 1969-70 on the basis of both these sets of aid figures are recorded in Table 1.4, which also relates performance to the average income in different donor countries. Although the share of aid in GNP for all DAC countries falls from 0.35% (on the conventional basis of net aid) to 0.32% (if interest payments are deducted) the relative rankings of individual donors are affected only to a minor extent. In 1969-70, donor rankings also show a remarkable similarity whether one takes disbursement net of both amortisation and interest, or the grant-equivalent value of commitments.

Terms of official aid commitments made in 1969 and 1970 improved somewhat over those made in 1968. Details are set out, by country, in Table 1.5.

′It still overstates the value of the transfer, particularly where aid is tied.

DAC continues to stress the importance of a further softening on terms through common efforts to harmonise towards those of the softer donors. The latest DAC Report makes a number of interesting new observations on the behaviour of donors in different situations. It notes, for example, that the major bilateral donor to any particular recipient country tends on the whole to provide aid on terms softer than the average of that of all donors combined; but it tends to be discouraged from even further softening by an unwillingness to see its aid being used for subsidising service payments to the fringe donors. DAC considers that the most hopeful approach to softer terms could come through a planned convergence of terms towards those of the major donor in any one recipient country, either through country based inter-donor consultations or through mutual agreement on the most appropriate terms for the recipient in question. This is a very useful suggestion.

Of the many conditions and restrictions which donors impose on their aid, procurement tying (in particular when it is combined with project tying and restrictions on the use of funds to the off-shore cost of projects) is the most generally contentious. The majority of donor countries now tie the bulk of their financial aid. No satisfactory empirical estimates of the ill-effects of tying have been made, but all the analytical evidence, supported by fragmentary statistical estimates as well as observation of individual aid operations, suggests that the loss of real value through the tying of aid can be substantial. While this problem has long been recognised, and inter-donor discussions on untying have proceeded almost as long, the general trend during the decade has been towards stricter and more extensive tying. Since Pearson, there have been new glimmers of hope : more countries have been willing to make exceptions (both in terms of local cost provision and procurement untying) in specific circumstances, and there has been a more liberal attitude on the issue of untying in favour of other developing countries. Discussions on the central issue of untying which had been going on under the auspices of DAC have been interrupted, however, in the aftermath of the Nixon measures. Further effort must depend for the time being on actions of other donors, although the observed trend towards more multilateral aid – which may receive another upward thrust from the US Congress – will automatically allow for some increase in the portion of aid which is not procurement tied.

DAC member contributions to multilateral agencies have increased much more quickly than bilateral official aid. The figures for DAC members as a group are shown in Table 1.6. After a drop in the middle of the decade – both in absolute terms and as a share of total aid – contributions to multilateral agencies have been rising very rapidly, to reach over 16% of total aid in 1970. On current estimates the

Table 1.4 Disbursements and Commitments of Official Development Assistance, Annual Average 1969-1970

	GNP per caput Average 1969–70 ($)	Disbursements Net of Amortisation and Interest			Commitments Grant Equivalent			(cf. Net of Amort. only)	
		Value ($m)	As % of GNP	Rank	Grant Equiv. Value ($m)	As % of GNP	Rank	% of GNP	Rank
Richest Four[1]									
1. US	4,700	2,945	0·29	11	2,869	0·29	11	0·32	10=
2. Sweden	3,700	118	0·38	5	151	0·48	5	0·41	5
3. Canada	3,500	294	0·37	6=	361	0·44	6	0·39	7
4. Switzerland	3,100	28	0·14	13	33	0·32	8	0·15	14
Middle Eight									
5. Denmark	2,900	56	0·37	6=	33	0·21	12	0·40	6
6. Norway	2,900	33	0·30	10	34	0·30	10	0·32	10=
7. Germany	2,800	526	0·31	9	571	0·31	9	0·36	9
8. France	2,800	918	0·63	1	1,034	0·70	1	0·67	1
9. Australia	2,600	189	0·56	2	218	0·63	2	0·56	3
10. Belgium	2,500	118	0·48	4	129	0·52	3=	0·50	4
11. Netherlands	2,300	165	0·54	3	163	0·52	3=	0·58	2
12. UK	2,100	381	0·33	8	415	0·34	7	0·38	8
Lowest Three[2]									
13. Austria	1,800	13	0·10	15	15	0·10	15	0·13	15
14. Japan	1,700	408	0·21	12	390	0·20	13	0·25	12
15. Italy	1,600	118	0·13	14	117	0·13	14	0·16	13
DAC Total	3,000	6,364	0·32	—	6,664	0·33	—	0·35	—

Notes: 1. Countries with an average income in excess of $3,000 (DAC average).
2. Countries with an average income below $2,000.

Source: *DAC Review 1971*, Annex I, Tables 1, 2, Statistical Tables 5, 6.

Table 1.5 Terms of Official Development Assistance Commitments, 1968-1970

	Gross Commitments $m			Grants as % of Total			Grant Equivalent %			Average Maturities Years			Av. Grace Period Years			Av. Interest %		
	1968	1969	1970	1968	1969	1970	1968	1969	1970	1968	1969	1970	1968	1969	1970	1968	1969	1970
Australia	219	218	235	100	100	91	100	100	93	—¹	—¹	14·0	—¹	—¹	4·0	—¹	—¹	6·4
Austria	22	21	24	51	69	41	64	79	58	11·9	14·6	13·9	1·9	4·2	4·2	5·1	4·4	5·1
Belgium	116	121	144	95	92	92	98	97	97	21·9	28·2	29·6	6·1	7·9	9·2	3·2	2·7	2·3
Canada	186	344	414	83	60	65	97	95	96	50·0	48·5	48·5	10·0	9·8	9·8	0	0·3	0·2
Denmark	81	89	63	57	76	92	90	95	98	24·9	25·0	25·0	7·0	7·0	7·0	0	0	0
France	1,305	1,239	1,232	72	74	73	81	84	83	17·6	17·0	16·2	1·7	1·9	2·3	3·7	3·7	3·7
Germany	607	642	810	51	51	54	74	77	80	23·4	26·0	27·5	7·1	7·6	8·5	3·0	3·2	2·9
Italy	193	244	190	30	27	54	50	43	68	12·3	10·2	13·1	2·3	1·8	5·2	4·7	5·3	4·9
Japan	329	564	593	62	42	39	80	68	67	17·9	19·5	21·4	5·6	6·1	6·7	3·7	3·7	3·7
Netherlands	250	173	206	52	69	64	74	87	85	27·9	28·6	29·0	6·4	8·1	7·8	3·8	3·1	2·9
Norway	27	30	41	92	91	99	97	97	99	23·0	36·0	23·0	5·5	7·9	9·0	2·2	1·7	2·4
Sweden	105	100	217	75	85	82	93	97	95	34·0	47·2	35·4	9·6	10·0	10·0	1·5	0·9	1·5
Switzerland	35	34	37	75	76	82	90	91	94	32·9	33·0	36·0	7·7	8·0	8·0	2·2	2·3	2·0
UK	560	487	526	46	48	50	82	82	82	24·0	24·1	24·6	5·6	5·6	6·2	1·0	1·2	1·7
US	4,032	3,292	3,342	54	70	64	84	89	87	38·0	37·1	37·4	9·0	8·7	8·7	2·6	3·0	2·6
All DAC	8,100	7,631	8,145	58	65	63	80	85	84	30·7	28·1	29·9	7·2	6·7	7·4	2·7	2·9	2·8

Note: 1. All aid in grant form.

Source: *DAC Review 1971*, Tables IV-1, 2.
DAC Review 1970, Tables III-1, 2.

26

Pearson target, that these contributions should reach at least 20% of total aid by 1975[1], may be reached. This expansion in the multilateral share is largely accounted for by the substantial second replenishment of IDA, which is reflected in the figures since 1968, and more recently by the rapid expansion of the operations of the Inter-American Development Bank and the emergence of other regional and sub-regional banks in Asia, Africa and the Caribbean into fully fledged lending institutions.

The contributions of individual DAC members in 1970 continue to reflect wide disparities. Australia (6.3%), Britain (10.6%) and France (10.8%) contributed the smallest shares in terms of their total aid disbursements. Norway, on the other hand, gave 60% of its aid through multilateral channels, with Sweden and Denmark not far behind with about 40% each : the Scandinavian preference for this form of aid was thus maintained. Austria, Belgium, Canada, Germany and the Netherlands also exceeded the 20% Pearson target.

Table 1.6   DAC Contributions to Multilateral Organisations, 1961-1970

Annual Averages	$m	Percentage in Total Official Development Assistance
1961–63	467	8
1964–66	362	6
1967–69	653	10
1970	1,124	16

Note: See Table 1.3 for figures showing total official development assistance, by country.
Source: *DAC Review 1971*, Table II-1.

Private Flows

Private commercial *capital* flows, as measured in international statistics, have shown a rapid increase over the decade as a whole. However, the figures do not take account of remittances of profits, interest and dividends. The effect of ignoring these transactions will vary from country to country. But for some, such as the UK, with substantial assets in the developing world and disincentives against new overseas investment, the return flow of profits and dividends may approach – or even exceed – the apparent 'net investment'. When using the figures for individual DAC member countries, shown in Tables 1.7 and 1.8, it must be remembered that they do not show the net *flow of resources* (as DAC implies) but rather the value of new capital exports, net of disinvestment and repaid export credits.

Table 1.7 shows that over the decade 1961-70 the four largest capital exporters were also the four largest contributors of official aid. For other countries, the respective rankings on overall aid and private flows were markedly different. Only Switzerland failed to record an absolute increase between the early and late sixties; and those showing

[1] *Partners in Development,* Report of the Commission on International Development ('Pearson Report'), 1969, p.215.

27

Table 1.7 Private Capital Flows (Net[1]) from DAC Countries to Developing Countries, 1961-1970

DAC Capital Exporters (Private)	Aid (ODA) Ranking on Overall Volume (1961–1970) (1)	Total			Annual Averages			
		Share in DAC (%) (2)	1961–1970 ($m) (3)	Col. (3) as a % of ODA (4)	1961–65 ($m) (5)	1966–70 ($m) (6)	1969–1970 only ($m) (7)	1969/70 as a % of ODA (8)
Big Five								
1. US	1	35·1	15,056	45	1,205	1,806	1,817	58
2. France	2	13·7	5,863	67	469	703	789	82
3. Germany	3	12·2	5,233	117	243	828	1,090	182
4. UK	4	10·8	4,600	102	409	511	750	170
5. Italy	8	7·8	3,382	345	232	462	632	455
		(79·6)						
Middle Six								
6. Japan	5	5·7	2,467	95	117	377	561	125
7. Switzerland	15	3·4	1,483	1,000	166	131	97	330
8. Netherlands	9	3·3	1,404	148	106	175	230	130
9. Belgium	10	2·4	1,040	113	86	122	126	107
10. Canada	6	1·4	625	42	34	90	123	42
11. Sweden	11	1·3	503	90	32	68	84	70
		(17·5)						
Little Four								
12. Australia	7	2·5	352	28	8	63	109	68
13. Austria	13		288	160	12	45	69	383
14. Denmark	12		236	99	11	36	67	117
15. Norway	14		171	102	11	23	32	94
DAC Total	—	100	42,796	(69%)	3,100 (54%[2])	5,460 (83%[2])	6,618	98%

Note: 1. Net of repayment (loans and credits) and disinvestment, but not of interest, dividends or profits.
2. As % of ODA.

Source: DAC Review 1971, Table II-1

28

the most substantial increase were Germany, Japan and, among smaller capital exporters, Australia, Austria and Denmark.

Within the total of private capital exports, direct investment almost doubled over the same period, while export credits trebled. More detailed figures are given in Table 1.8.

Table 1.8   Summary of DAC Total Private Capital Flows to Developing Countries 1960-1970[1]

	Annual Average 1960–1965	1966	1967	1968	1969	1970
Direct Investment	1,830	2,180	2,110	3,050	2,700	3,010
Portfolio and Other	620	660	1,270	1,740	1,800	1,150
Export Credits	660	1,120	1,000	1,590	1,980	2,170
Total	3,110	3,960	4,380	6,380	6,480	6,730

$m (header above table)

Note: 1. Net of capital repayments and disinvestment, but not of interest and dividends.
Source: DAC Review 1971, Table VI-1.

The 1971 DAC Review estimates that export credits will continue to increase more rapidly than other types of private capital flow, reaching perhaps around $3.5 billion by 1975 compared with $5.5 billion for other private flows. DAC also estimates that compliance by all members with the 1% target on official and private 'flows' combined would require a total resource flow of some $25.5 billion[1] by 1975. The estimated value of private 'flows' in 1975 would be equivalent to roughly 0.3% of the combined GNP of DAC members. This has one very important implication for the UN 1% target, which all DAC countries have accepted. Whatever individual countries feel about the separate 0.7% target for official aid alone, as a group they will not be able to reach the 1% target by 1975 unless they can step up their combined official aid contribution to an amount equivalent to 0.7% of their GNP.

[1] At 1970 prices.

2 British Aid

ODM's Absorption into the FCO

The most immediate concern of the British aid lobby, during the first few months following the 1970 General Election, was the future of the Ministry of Overseas Development (ODM).

ODM was set up in 1964, by the newly-elected Labour Government, as a further step in the process of rationalisation which began in 1961 when a new Department of Technical Co-operation was established with responsibility for co-ordinating technical assistance. ODM took over the functions of that Department and was also made responsible for all capital aid. Budgetary aid to the remaining colonies continued to be administered by the Colonial Office (which was subsequently merged into the Commonwealth Office and later amalgamated with the Foreign Office), and Britain's relations with the World Bank continued to be primarily a Treasury responsibility; but with these exceptions, ODM managed the whole British aid programme. Its first Minister (Mrs. Castle) was included in the Cabinet, and this was widely taken as a sign that development assistance was to be given a new priority.

There were rumours, however, during the last three years of Labour Government, that ODM was in danger of losing its autonomy and of being reabsorbed into another department. These did not come to anything : but the Conservative Government elected in June 1970 was explicitly pledged to streamlining the Whitehall framework; and although initially ODM continued as a separate ministry, there was soon more confident speculation that it might be merged with the Foreign and Commonwealth Office or the Board of Trade -- or that it might even be split between the two. There was heated debate, spreading through Parliament's summer recess, concerning the practical and psychological importance of maintaining a separate aid ministry. Even ODM's strongest defenders had to confess that the Ministry had already been effectively down-graded in 1967, when the Minister had ceased to have a regular seat in the Cabinet; but it was pointed out that although Britain was unusual in having a separate aid ministry, the administrative structure of the British aid programme was the envy of many other members of DAC. In the six years of its existence, ODM had been able to build up a skilled cadre of professional aid administrators and specialists; and the Estimates Committee on Overseas Aid had reported, in October 1968 :

> 'There can be little doubt from the evidence that the British
> aid programme has become much more effective in the last

30

few years, and that credit for this must go to the Ministry of Overseas Development.'

The Committee added that 'To merge the Ministry of Overseas Development in one vast overseas department' would be a 'retrograde' step. An independent Minister, even one outside the Cabinet, was said to be in a better position to defend the interests of long-term development, in cases where these were not precisely aligned with Britain's shorter-term political and commercial interests; and it was also held to be important, at the official level, that inter-departmental arguments should be pursued by members of an independent ministry. The Government was urged to reconstitute the Select Committee on Overseas Aid, which had been unable to submit its report before the previous Parliament was dissolved, and to await the Committee's recommendations before making its decision; but the basic principle had probably already been decided, and in October it was announced[1] that ODM would cease to operate as a separate ministry and would become instead a 'functional wing' of the Foreign and Commonwealth Office. On 12 November, the Overseas Develoment Administration (ODA) became effective as a distinct department within the FCO.

It was inevitable that the very fact of the merger should be seen, both in Britain and abroad, as an indication that British aid policy was to become more closely integrated with general foreign policy. On the other hand, it is arguable that aid is in any case just one aspect of foreign policy, and even that, having once ceased to have special representation in Cabinet, ODA is better served by having direct access to Cabinet through the Foreign and Commonwealth Secretary. In any case, those who had been advocating the retention of a separate ministry were reassured in so far as the new arrangement did not involve any substantive changes in the running of the aid programme. Concerning policy formulation, it is hard to tell whether the merger has in itself enabled or contributed to a re-orientation of criteria; every government has different priorities, and even if the geographical distribution of aid seems to become more heavily influenced by political and commercial objectives, a re-orientation of this sort could easily have been effected without any change in the formal status of ODM.

Colonial Administration

Prior to 1970, the FCO (as successor to the Colonial Office) looked after British colonial policy, but colonial aid and technical assistance was administered by ODM. Subsequently, during ODA's first year as a department within the FCO, administration of Britain's 18 remaining colonies continued to be shared between different offices; but at the end

'*The Reorganisation of Central Government*, Cmnd. 4506, HMSO, October 1971.

of 1971 a new joint department, the Joint Dependent Territories Division (DTD), was set up to deal with colonial aid work as well as general policy and administration. The staff was drawn partly from ODA and partly from elsewhere within the FCO.

The DTD deals with aid questions according to usual ODA procedures; it has access to ODA advisers and others as necessary; and its establishment may be seen as a logical step which will permit the faster and more efficient administration of British aid amounting to some £20m per year.

Report of the Select Committee on Overseas Aid

At virtually the same time that it published its decision concerning the future of ODM, the Government announced its intention to reconstitute the Select Committee on Overseas Aid. This Committee had first been appointed in April 1969. Re-appointed for the 1969-70 Session, it had still been unable to draft its report before Parliament was dissolved; and the new Committee was therefore appointed, in December 1970, to examine and report upon the evidence submitted to its predecessors. It had no power to take further evidence; and its report[1], based on evidence taken between nine months and two years previously, was published in March 1971.

The Committee was mainly concerned with the objectives, size and cost of the aid programme, and with management of bilateral aid. It also paid particular attention to the need for an improved British effort to aid rural development; and further sections in the report were devoted to aid relationships (both with recipients and with other donors), multilateral aid, the Commonwealth Development Corporation, private investment, trade, the Voluntary Agencies, and publicity for the aid programme. The speed with which the new Committee – despite the change in the balance of its composition – was able to complete its report, suggests that its members were in broad agreement on almost all these issues.

After a further three months, the Minister published a White Paper[2] in which he commented on each of the Committee's 64 principle recommendations. He refused to accept the most fundamental of the Committee's proposals – concerning the basic size of the aid programme; but on most other topics, his comments – even where he did not immediately accept the Committee's views – at least indicated that the proposals were being given full consideration.

On the size of the aid programme, the Committee believed that

[1]*Report from the Select Committee on Overseas Aid,* Session 1970-71, HC 299, HMSO.
[2]*Report from the Select Committee on Overseas Aid: Observations by the Minister for Overseas Development,* Cmnd. 4687, HMSO, June 1971.

32

expenditure should cease to be subject to a ceiling fixed in cash terms; and they recommended that:

> 'Future expenditure on aid should be fixed as a percentage of gross national product or, if this is not practicable, as a percentage of public expenditure.'

In response, the Minister merely observed[1] that,

> 'The Government have not accepted a commitment to provide any specific percentage of GNP in the form of official aid',

adding that it would not be relevant either to any recognised target for aid or to the purposes of development assistance to determine the aid programme as a percentage of public expenditure. Since they were not included in the summary of the Committee's recommendations, the Minister was able to ignore the Committee's reference to the 1% target as a minimum figure, and their view that,

> 'The Pearson target of 0.7% of GNP for official aid should be fulfilled[2].'

There were a number of matters on which the Minister was not able, at the time, to give a definite answer. Two – concerning the carryover of unspent ODA balances from one financial year to the next and the improvement of aid management overseas – have since been clarified by separate announcements[3]; but there are several other points on which the aid lobby would welcome a more positive response. In particular:

> (1) If the Government wishes to improve its effort to aid rural development, it should reconsider its attitude towards finance of local costs (which at present are met only 'in exceptional circumstances'), and also towards expansion of both the Tropical Products Institute and the Corps of Specialists.
>
> (2) Despite the present hiatus in the OECD discussions following last year's international monetary crisis, the Government could re-examine the possibility of an independent initiative towards reduced tying of bilateral aid.
>
> (3) The Government could – at the 1972 review of the IMF's Special Drawing Rights scheme – increase its efforts towards an agreement which would link the future allocation of SDRs with development assistance.
>
> (4) On trade, the Government could pursue more actively its stated policy[4], 'to reduce, wherever possible, tariff and non-tariff

[1]Cmnd. 4687, para 10.
[2]HC (1970-71) 299, para 52. See also p. 25 above.
[3]See p. 46.
[4]Cmnd. 4687, para 64.

barriers to trade with developing countries and to encourage other developed countries to pursue similar policies'. Trade liberalism will need to be linked with appropriate domestic policies to soften the immediate effects, from increased competition, on local industries.

(5) Having rejected the Committee's proposal that it should set up a further Select Committee on Overseas Aid, the Government has an increased responsibility to see that sufficient Parliamentary time is set aside for regular discussion of the aid programme.

(6) Having accepted the need for a better informed public opinion concerning the aid programme, the Government may need to increase its financial support to the informational work both of the Voluntary Agencies and of ODA's own Information Department.

Recent Aid Performance

In money terms, the volume of net new aid flowing from Britain to developing countries varied remarkably little throughout the 1960s (see Table 2.1); and because of inflation, the value of British aid, in terms of purchasing power for recipient countries, fell substantially. 1970 was therefore most significant for the fact that the volume of gross official flows was decisively increased, away from the £210m mark. The figures for net aid (both for 'net official flows', as defined by UNCTAD, and for the amount remaining after deduction of interest as well as capital repayments) were also new records.

Nevertheless, the 1970 net aid flow represented, compared to 1969, an even smaller proportion of British gross national product. According to international criteria, British aid performance therefore continued to decline : net official aid, expressed as a percentage of GNP, slumped during the last decade from 0.59% in 1961 to 0.37% in 1970. Britain is now little more than half way towards the 0.7% target which was proposed in the Pearson Report and which has since been adopted (but not by Britain) as part of the UN strategy for the Second Development Decade. In both 1969 and 1970, on the other hand, Britain reached the UN 1% target for the total of official and private flows taken together. The Government, while accepting the 1% target, has still not undertaken the 0.7% target for official aid alone, nor even accepted the need for a separate official aid target : the relative importance of the two targets – and particularly the question whether private and official flows are as interchangeable as the Government's attitude implies – is discussed further in Chapter 3.

Concerning official flows, it will be seen that reverse flows of amortisation and interest, after increasing rapidly between 1960 and 1965, have tended to level off in the last few years. The terms of British aid have been substantially improved since the introduction, in 1965, of interest-free loans; and of total British aid disbursed in 1970 (£219m), 48% (including bilateral technical assistance and contributions to multilateral agencies, £46m and £7m respectively) was disbursed in the form of grants. An additional 42% was lent on interest-free terms and 6% took the form of overseas investment by CDC.

Table 2.1   Total Net Flow of Resources from Britain to Developing Countries, 1961-1970
£m

	1961	1962	1963	1964	1965	1966	1967	1968	1969	1970
Official flows[1]										
Gross	172·6	164·7	164·3	194·8	197·3	213·5	208·4	210·6	210·5	218·8
deduct capital repayments	10·4	10·7	15·6	18·3	24·0	30·3	29·4	32·2	32·0	29·9
Net	162·2	154·0	148·7	176·5	173·3	183·2	179·0	178·5	178·5	188·9
deduct interest received	11·1	12·3	20·4	23·8	26·2	27·7	28·2	27·7	28·4	29·3
New net aid	151·1	141·7	128·3	152·7	147·1	155·5	150·9	150·8	150·1	159·7
Private flows										
Investment (net)[2]	131·0	75·5	73·4	100·2	157·0	95·0	77·0	70·0	188·0	136·0
Export credits (net)[3]	25·9	37·7	34·4	51·3	38·3	47·1	41·3	58·1	110·8	181·8
Voluntary Organisations	..	..	..	..	..	..	..	..	..	19·0[4]
Total (net)	156·9	113·2	107·9	151·5	195·3	142·1	118·3	128·1	298·8	336·8
Total net flows	319·1	267·2	256·6	328·0	368·6	325·3	297·3	306·6	477·3	525·7
Net flows as a percentage of gross national product[5]										
Official	0·59	0·53	0·48	0·53	0·48	0·48	0·45	0·42	0·39	0·37
Private	0·57	0·39	0·35	0·45	0·55	0·37	0·30	0·30	0·65	0·67
Total	1·16	0·92	0·84	0·98	1·03	0·84	0·74	0·71	1·04	1·04

.. Not available.

Notes: 1. Figures for 1961–63 are on an unadjusted basis. Since 1964 they have been adjusted to show CDC investments rather than borrowing from the Exchequer.
2. Net of disinvestment by UK residents or companies, but not of profit and dividend remittances.
3. Private export credits under official guarantee and with maturities in excess of 1 year. Net of capital repayments, but not of interest.
4. Estimated grants by private voluntary agencies.
5. According to the latest UNCTAD definition.
Source: British Aid Statistics, HMSO.

A new pattern of interest rates was introduced in July 1970. Most loans continue to be interest-free; but interest-bearing loans, instead of being made at the Government lending rate softened where necessary by waivers, are now made at fixed concessionary rates ranging from 2% to 7½%. The stated object of the new arrangement is merely to enable Britain, where appropriate, to match loan terms more closely to those provided by other members of DAC lending to the same recipient. More important, only 10% of new loan commitments signed in 1970 bore any interest; and 99% carried a grace period for capital repayments. Total new commitments in 1970 amounted to £220m, of which £108 m (49%) was in grant form and £112m was in loans. Overall, the combined weighted grant element of 1970 commitments, excluding

35

investment by CDC, was officially estimated to be equivalent to £174m; and Britain's performance on terms satisfied fairly comfortably the new target recommendations introduced by DAC, as a measure of international comparison, in 1969.

In one respect, British aid performance in 1970 deteriorated : there was a significant increase in the extent to which aid was tied to the purchase of British goods and services. Leaving aside the cost of technical assistance and certain categories of financial aid to which the tied-untied distinction is not strictly applicable, 48% of 1970 British bilateral aid, compared to 43% in 1969, was completely tied. It is also estimated[1] that the purchases of British goods and services, arising from the tying of some other aid to British or local recipient procurement, corresponded to a further 16% of the total (as against only 11% in 1969). The effective degree of tying, irrespective of any British orders which might have been financed by untied aid, was therefore 64%, i.e. 10% more than in 1969.

This increase in tying was not known to the Select Committee, which nevertheless drew attention to the additional benefits which would accrue to recipient countries if British aid were not tied. The Committee considered that, because of the prospective loss to Britain's competitive position, it would not be politically feasible for Britain to untie her bilateral aid unless other donors did the same; and they therefore took the view that Britain should concentrate on efforts to reach an international agreement for reduced tying. Britain and other members of DAC have in fact been engaged in drafting a scheme for reciprocal untying of contributions to multilateral agencies and of bilateral loans; but work on the scheme has temporarily been discontinued. Meanwhile, Britain might reconsider the possibility of untying bilateral aid : an independent initiative, in addition to enabling a substantial improvement to the quality of British aid, would have important diplomatic value.

The untying of British aid would enable more effective emphasis to be placed on the priority sectors, which have been identified[2] as agriculture, 'insofar as this is appropriate within the development plans and policies of the recipient', technical education and manpower planning. Over the five-year period 1966-70, out of total British commitments of project aid (£373m) only 12% was for renewable natural resources, including agriculture, and 11% was for social infrastructure (including health as well as education). While it is true that a redistribution of British aid towards the priority sectors could only be effected if it were consistent with recipient wishes, the British Government could at least state, more explicitly, that it is willing to

[1] *An Account of the British Aid Programme*, HMSO, 1971, **para 55.**
[2] Ibid. para 66.

36

co-operate in such a redistribution. The Select Committee particularly urged that :

> 'Assistance to rural development projects which are economically sound should not be inhibited on account of local costs';

to which the Minister merely replied, equivocally :

> 'Local costs are met only in exceptional circumstances and to a limited extent but the British Government may need to meet some local cost element if it is a major donor, or where aid is being given for rural development and other projects of high economic priority.'

A more positive attitude towards financing of local costs might be an important factor in facilitating fruitful dialogue, through British Missions, at the project planning stage. An improved contribution from the Missions, in their exchanges with ODA as well as with recipient governments, will also substantially depend on the increased availability to them of suitable expertise; and in this regard the establishment of three new development divisions is an important step forward[1].

There is a fundamentally more unsatisfactory aspect of the aid programme, second only to the programme's small size, in so far as there still appears to be no coherent strategy behind either the overall qualitative distribution of aid or the geographical allocation of aid as between different countries. The 1970 submission to DAC again merely reported that :

> 'Criteria for the allocation of aid remained unchanged during the year, and the distribution of the British aid programme continued to lay emphasis on multilateral aid and technical assistance and on Britain's special obligation to the Dependencies[2].'

The main weakness in aid planning concerns the geographical allocation of bilateral aid, particularly financial aid, as between different countries. Before examining this further, however, we shall consider four other main categories of aid which – partly because their respective disbursements are more easily forecast – are in practice given first call on whatever sum is available for the programme as a whole. These are multilateral aid, technical assistance, loans to CDC, and pensions to former British expatriate officers.

With reference to the declared emphasis on multilateral aid, it may

[1]See p.46.
[2]*An Account of the British Aid Programme*, para 62.

37

be observed that in 1970 Britain's contributions to multilateral agencies, £19.8m, were smaller as a percentage of her total net aid (10.6%) than the corresponding proportion for any other DAC members except Australia and Portugal. On the other hand, Britain has played an important and constructive role in promoting the third IDA replenishment (which, however, cannot become effective until it is ratified by the United States); and with regard to a bigger contribution to the UN system, the Government has at least already stated its position, believing that further reform along the lines proposed in the Jackson Report can best be encouraged by agreeing to increase resources 'as and when the organisations show their ability to make effective use of additional funds'[1].

The Government has found it easier to fulfil its policy commitment towards technical assistance. Total bilateral technical assistance disbursements have increased steadily in recent years, from £30.4m (17% of the gross bilateral programme) in 1965 to £45.6m (just over 25%) in 1970 : 61% of the 1970 disbursements was for finance of experts and volunteers, and a further 19% represented finance for students and trainees in Britain. The Government is attempting to improve the quality of technical assistance by evolving an administrative framework which is more sensitive to the requirements of aid recipients. New technical assistance agreements signed with overseas governments provide for annual reviews of the expected needs for British staff; and it is intended that these annual discussions will also cover other complementary forms of manpower aid, such as training.

The largest number of appointments made under various technical assistance arrangements continues to be in the field of education; but, in general, increasing emphasis is being placed on filling posts of high developmental value. ODA is experiencing increasing difficulty in meeting the demands for some specialists, particularly in agriculture, medicine, economics, finance and land survey : the Corps of Specialists provides continuity of employment, for periods of up to ten years, for some seventy experts, particularly in administration, finance, agriculture and engineering, but although the number of tropical agriculturist posts has recently been doubled from fifteen to thirty, the Corps's overall size and composition, as well as the conditions of service offered to its members, need to be kept under constant review. ODA's ability to react promptly to overseas requests would also be significantly improved if the Tropical Products Institute, together with the department's other scientific out-stations, were exempted from the restrictions that apply generally to the expansion of Civil Service manpower.

The Government is giving increasing support to the Commonwealth Development Corporation. The Select Committee reported favourably

[1]Cmnd. 4687, para 31.

on CDC's performance, and made a number of detailed recommendations concerning ways in which the Corporation's activities might be facilitated or improved. Most of these were sympathetically received, except that Government declined to examine the possibility of allowing CDC to have a revolving fund, on the grounds that such a fund would involve a fundamental change in the Corporation's financial structure. Public lending to CDC was increased from £11m in 1969/70 to £15m in 1970/71, and it is understood that the Corporation is now being given a clearer indication, up to three or four years in advance, concerning the amounts of money which will be at its disposal in future[1].

If CDC is to be assigned an increasingly important role in the general British aid effort – and this would seem to be in line with current Government thinking – it will be correspondingly more important for CDC's investments to be distributed where they will make the maximum contribution to development. CDC's policy in this respect is stated quite clearly in its 1970 Annual Report :

> 'CDC does not choose its investments either for maximum commercial return or for the greatest assistance to United Kingdom exports. It does choose them for their development value to the country concerned, provided that the projects are viable in themselves.'

Nevertheless, in view of the fact that in both 1969 and 1970 about half of CDC's new investments were in the Caribbean region (mainly in tourism), it may be asked whether the Corporation is presently putting too much emphasis on safe commercial reward and also, perhaps, taking an unduly pessimistic view as to the political safety of investing in other areas.

The Select Committee made two recommendations concerning the pattern of CDC's new investments. First, that 'CDC should reconsider the needs of India and Pakistan in the fields of agriculture and rural development', at which the Minister rightly observed that this was primarily a matter for consideration by CDC itself; and second, that 'in selecting new countries for investment the CDC should keep in mind Britain's competitive position in countries which in the years ahead are going to provide important markets'. With regard to the second recommendation the Minister responded, more substantively :

> 'Before investing in new countries the CDC look at the situation as a whole, including the effect on British interests. The Minister will have similar considerations in mind before reaching a decision on any applications by the CDC to begin operations in new countries.'

[1]Cmnd. 4687, para 51.

This suggests that there may be some policy ambiguity, at least within Government, concerning the future geographical spread of CDC's investments; and it should be noted that although project proposals are formally initiated by CDC itself, any project whose total cost exceeds £250,000 requires Government approval.

The fourth aid category which in practice is regarded as a priority call on the programme as a whole, is the payment of pensions for former British expatriate civil servants; but there are strong arguments for the exclusion of this category from the official aid programme. It was announced in March 1970 that Britain would be willing, if requested, to assume responsibility as from April 1971 for pensions payable by overseas governments in respect of pre-independence government service by British staff. The Select Committee drew attention to the fact that other former colonial powers accept an analogous responsibility, and also that France, Belgium and Italy do not count the payments as part of their aid programme (while the Netherlands includes some but not others). While agreeing with the Government view that assumption of such a responsibility by Britain should be taken into account when determining the amount of aid to be allocated to a particular country, the Committee accordingly recommended that the pensions paid by Britain should be excluded from British aid flows[1]. The Minister rejected this proposal, merely adding that the payments would be in grant form and that they would relieve overseas governments of payments which they now make, thus freeing foreign exchange for other purposes. He thus disregarded the Select Committee's opinion that it was inequitable for former British colonies to have had to meet the payments concerned in the first place; and the new arrangement (involving Exchequer transfers to British subjects most of whom now live in Britain) clearly does not satisfy the new DAC test of official development assistance flows that they should be administered 'with, as the main objective, the promotion of the economic development and welfare of developing countries'[2]. By the end of November 1971, twenty-one governments had given notice that they wished to take advantage of the British offer as it stands; but this response, although it represents an acknowledgement that the new system is an improvement, in no way indicates that the present compromise is satisfactory.

There remains the question of the geographical distribution of the bilateral aid programme. For historical reasons, much the greater part of British bilateral aid continues to go to Commonwealth countries, which in 1970 received gross disbursements of £171.8m – 89% of the total bilateral programme (£193.9m). Among the Commonwealth

[1]HC (1970-71) 299, para 29.
[2]DAC Review 1971, p.146.

countries, the smaller ones – particularly when compared to India and Pakistan – tend to receive much greater amounts of aid per head[1].

The Select Committee included in its Report a conventional analysis of the difficulty of changing the existing distribution pattern; but even if one acknowledges Britain's special responsibility towards the remaining dependencies, and admits both that the concentration on Commonwealth countries will continue for some time to come and that 'Aid cannot be turned on and off like a tap', one may still dispute the Committee's conclusion that 'greater flexibility can only be achieved by increasing the aid budget'. Although it is true that disbursements in any particular year are largely determined by commitments entered into in previous years, it must still be asked whether the Government has operated an effective system for continual review and comparison of different countries' needs and deserts. An historically inherited pattern can all too easily become self-perpetuating.

Now that the aid programme is to be expanded, the criteria for geographical allocation will become correspondingly more important. R. B. M. King, Deputy Secretary in ODA, explained in a recent paper[2] that three main groups of factors – developmental, political and commercial – are taken into account in planning the aid framework; but it is clearly not possible to generalise about the relative importance which is ascribed to developmental factors as against the others.

There cannot even be any hard and fast rules for comparing the purely developmental needs of different countries. But while it is practically impossible to ignore some basic political considerations, there is at least a prima facie case, in the design of an 'aid' programme, for leaving out commercial considerations altogether. The Select Committee distinguished between the 'needy' (i.e. those countries having the greatest need for aid) and the 'speedy' (those with the most efficient machinery for making use of aid); and underlined both the arbitrariness of the 'inevitable' compromise and the extent of current confusion concerning allocation criteria, by concluding that:

> 'As the ceiling increases, more emphasis should be placed on assisting the "speedy" (some of whom will be the donor countries of the future) in cases where this would stimulate commercial interests but . . . not . . . that this should be done at the expense of the truly "needy".'

More significant, perhaps, was the Committee's opinion that, in an enlarged aid programme, increased attention should be paid to the problems of India and Pakistan.

[1] The regional distribution of British aid, 1966-1969 (average) and 1970, is shown in Table 1 of Appendix A. Tables A.2 and A.3 list the 29 countries which received the highest gross British aid in 1966-1970, indicating the amounts of aid received per head and the breakdown of aid by various categories.
[2] R.B.M. King, *The Planning of the British Aid Programme*, ODA, June 1971.

Aid Management

Important announcements were made, in 1971, of two major changes which should lead to significant improvements in the management of the British aid programme. Both are consistent with recommendations made by the Select Committee.

The first, announced in June, will enable what was previously an aid ceiling to be regarded more as a target. Up to and including 1970/71, the aid programme was fixed as a gross annual cash sum which could not be exceeded. In these circumstances, there was always the danger, in any financial year, that either the allocation would be under-spent – in which case the money would be permanently 'lost' (in the sense that the following year's allocation would not be correspondingly increased) – or that there might be a temptation to relax approval procedures in order to ensure that the money was spent in time. The new arrangement, on the other hand, will enable ODA – subject to Parliamentary authority – to exceed the aid programme total for any year by up to £5m. In addition, it will be possible – subject to the approval of the Treasury – to carry over into the following year any under-spending which is judged to have resulted from action or inaction on the part of other Governments or international organisations. Such carryover would normally be limited to about £5m in any one year; but the Minister will be willing 'to consider with other [Treasury] Ministers the possibility of making good a larger short-fall over more than one succeeding year'.

Second, and more important in the long term, it was announced in November 1971 that three new Development Divisions were to be set up – in East Africa, Southern Africa and South-East Asia respectively – to join the Divisions already existing in the Middle East and the Caribbean. This will enable significant decentralisation of aid management to people more closely on the spot.

Up to now the British aid programme has largely been administered from London, through diplomatic Missions, backed up by visits from ODA specialists based in the United Kingdom. ODA staff have occasionally been posted to diplomatic Missions for longer periods; but Missions have generally lacked the expertise needed to deal with the many problems that arise in the course of planning and implementing country aid programmes. Decisions were taken, in London, without the up-to-date and first-hand knowledge of recipient problems which can only be gained from residence in the area; and Missions were not in a position to give expert help in the identification of useful areas for assistance, or with the preparation, appraisal and implementation of projects.

The Select Committee noted in its report that the quality of the British aid programme could be greatly increased by the appointment of more aid specialists to overseas Missions, and added that, in some areas, expertise might be provided more effectively and economically through the creation of more Development Divisions.

Development Divisions are formally regional offices of ODA, staffed by small groups of development specialists, whose main duties are to provide consultancy services and technical assistance to governments that require it, and to advise British diplomatic Missions on the scope, make-up and use of individual country aid programmes. The two older Divisions are respectively sited in Beirut and Barbados; and the latter, in addition to serving the Commonwealth Caribbean, administers aid directly in the Associated States and remaining dependencies, with delegated authority to approve capital aid projects costing not more than £250,000. The three new Divisions will be in Nairobi (covering Kenya, Uganda, Zambia, Mauritius, Seychelles and possibly, if Britain undertakes new aid commitments there, Tanzania); Blantyre (provisionally for Malawi, Botswana, Lesotho and Swaziland); and Bangkok (probably covering Indonesia, Malaysia, Singapore, Philippines, Thailand and Burma). When fully operational, the five Divisions will cover some 50 countries or territories, which between them accounted for about 45% (£90m) of 1970 British bilateral aid.

The Select Committee, noting the authority delegated to the Caribbean Division, recommended that there should be a degree of delegation to all British Missions which can call on the type of expertise provided by Development Divisions. It is now possible to implement this recommendation in a larger number of countries. There remains the question of how to improve the quality of the British aid programme in countries which are still not covered by Development Divisions. Of the four countries which each received, in 1970, gross British aid amounting to more than £10m, only one, Kenya, is included in a Development Division area. Aid to India, Pakistan and Nigeria, and also to other large recipients such as Ghana and Ceylon, will continue to be administered from London.

The Minister for Overseas Development wrote in his Observations on the Select Committee Report that, 'The importance of making available more specialist advice to Missions overseas is fully appreciated, and various methods of achieving this are being examined.' The new Development Divisions will greatly facilitate the planning and administration of the aid programme in about fifteen countries; but urgent consideration still needs to be given to the needs of Missions elsewhere.

3 British Development Policy

British development policy must be seen as a single entity, which not only embraces aid and other economic relationships between Britain and the developing countries but also is inextricably bound up with other aspects of British foreign policy. The Conservative Party's statement on aid and development policy, in its 1970 General Election manifesto, stated that :

> 'Britain must play a proper part in dealing with world poverty. We will ensure that Britain helps the developing countries :
>
>> by working for the expansion of international trade;
>> by encouraging private investment overseas;
>> by providing capital aid and technical assistance to supplement their own efforts.'

At least in principle, the Government thus does see its policy towards developing countries as an integrated whole. This approach, which is gaining ground in other donor countries as well as Britain, has partly been brought about by pressures from the developing countries themselves, particularly through UNCTAD and ECOSOC : and it is ironic, therefore, that agreement on international targets for non-trade resource flows has tended to blur the distinctions between the different types of flow and in some respects, by focusing on overall quantity rather than on direction and quality, has diverted attention away from the developing countries' own needs.

In practice, it is difficult for Britain to have an integrated development policy so long as ODA continues to be almost exclusively concerned with aid administration. Particularly with regard to developing countries' trade, there would at least need to be greater consultation and co-operation between the Department of Trade and Industry and ODA. The latter does now have a special adviser on private investment[1]; but partly because of the attitude which Government has taken towards the UNCTAD targets, there is considerable confusion within Britain about the relationship between private investment and aid and, moreover, as to what private 'investment' actually embraces. The present chapter will mainly be concerned to remove some of this confusion and – since the reality of an integrated development policy does not yet exist – to examine the Government's separate policies towards

[1] A new Private Investment and Consultancies Department has recently been established in ODA. This, in addition to bringing together some of the work hitherto done under these headings in other departments, will provide, for the first time, a definite point of contact for private sector approaches to ODA.

aid, private investment and trade, respectively. The chapter concludes with a brief examination of what would be implied in any attempt to adopt a more truly integrated British development policy.

The UN Targets[1]

Speaking at the United Nations 25th anniversary celebrations in October 1970, the Prime Minister said :

'I reaffirm our acceptance of the 1% target agreed at the second UNCTAD conference in 1968. In accordance with the strategy for the second (development) decade we shall do our best to reach the target by 1975.'

Even to those who see useful significance in the 1% target, this must have seemed a rather hollow undertaking when it was learnt, soon after the Prime Minister's speech, that in the previous year, for the first time since 1965, total financial flows from Britain to developing countries had in fact slightly exceeded 1% of our GNP. In 1970, Britain reached the target again.

On the other hand, Britain has *not* undertaken the UN 0.7% target for official aid alone; and it should therefore be recalled that the main reason for Pearson's proposal of a separate target for official development assistance was that the original UNCTAD 1% target 'is not, strictly speaking, an aid target at all'[2]. The blanket 1% makes no differentiation between commercial transactions and official aid; and official aid, since it is deliberately conceived as development assistance and is therefore able to provide a reliable flow of resources, on concessional terms, to sectors of high priority to the recipients' development, 'merits more attention than the 1% target accords to it'.

The British position with regard to the 0.7% target was formally stated in a submission[3] to the UN Committee on International Development Strategy : 'The United Kingdom Government accepts that official flows of development assistance should form a substantial part of total flows . . . (but) does not accept the need for a separate target for official development assistance.' It is much to be regretted that Britain, while joining in the adoption of the overall UN strategy for the Second Development Decade, was thus unable to accept the most important target set for developed countries in that strategy.

The Official Aid Programme

The Government has at least, however, committed itself to expanding the official aid programme, at a rate which is roughly in line with

[1]See pp.25 and 37.
[2]Pearson Report, p.147.
[3]*An International Development Strategy for the Second United Nations Development Decade,* Cmnd. 4568, HMSO, 1971.

proposals originally announced by the Labour Government in November 1969.

Moreover, the presentation of the latest projections is substantially improved. Most important, instead of being expressed in cash terms, at out-turn prices, the figures are shown at constant 1971 prices, and there will therefore no longer be a danger of the real value of proposed increases being swallowed up by inflation. The figures are also, for the first time, shown net of amortisation receipts from past loans (although there is still no allowance for interest payments); and it is explained in the White Paper[1] that the aid programme will in future be determined on a net constant price basis, with each annual programme being converted to a gross cash sum for the submission of the Estimates to Parliament. There is an additional small but overdue change in classification, in that special defence aid to Malaysia and Singapore has been transferred from 'Overseas Aid' to another heading, 'Other Military Defence'.

Finally, there is one important policy change, in that the estimate for the new financial year, 1972-73, is £9m higher than the figure which is arrived at by merely revaluing the corresponding figure which appeared in the previous Public Expenditure review[2]. The estimates for the two following years correspond almost exactly to the figures in the previous review; and the estimate for 1975-76 represents a further 9% increase on that for 1974-75. Net official flows to developing countries are expected to rise to £290m in 1975-76. This represents an average annual percentage increase, between 1971-72 and 1975-76, of 7.6%, compared to an estimated average annual percentage increase, over the same period, for public expenditure as a whole, of only 2.7%. Detailed figures are set out in Table 3.1.

Table 3.1 British Aid: Current Flows and Future Estimates, 1970-1976

£m, at 1971 Prices

	Provisional Out-turn	Current and Future Estimates				
	1970–71	1971–72	1972–73	1973–74	1974–75	1975–76
a. Aid Programme[1]	205·3	214·1	231·9	243·0	265	289
b. Other Net Investment by CDC	0·7	1·7	2·6	2·2	1	1
c. Total Public Expenditure on Overseas Aid[2]	206·0	215·8	234·5	245·2	266	290

Notes: 1. Net of capital repayments, but not of interest.
2. The aid programme (line a) includes advances from the Exchequer to CDC net of repayments; the public expenditure figures (line c) incorporate the net flow of funds from CDC to overseas countries. The adjustment (line b) represents the difference between the two figures.
Source: Cmnd. 4829, Table 2.3.

The new estimates have received a measured welcome from the aid lobby. There is some comfort in the fact that, having declined to

[1]*Public Expenditure to 1975-76*, Cmnd. 4829, HMSO, November 1971.
[2]*Public Expenditure 1969-70 to 1974-75*, Cmnd. 4578, HMSO, January 1971.

relate the aid programme to GNP, the Government has ignored the Select Committee's recommendation[1] that, alternatively, aid should merely be fixed as a percentage of total public expenditure. Nevertheless, it is clear that, even if one assumes a British rate of growth of only 2% per annum over the period, British aid in 1975-76 will still represent not more than about 0.5% of our GNP. If the British growth-rate is 4%, British aid in 1975-76 will be only about 0.45% of GNP.

It is also to be regretted that the White Paper projections still make no allowance for receipts of interest on past loans. The Select Committee suggested that Britain should seek to ensure that in future the UNCTAD classification of aid should make allowance for interest payments received by the donor country; but the Government, despite the fact that the great majority of British lending is now interest-free, considered that the UNCTAD classification should continue to relate merely to net capital flows. It must be admitted that deduction of *all* return payments would provide a more realistic measure of the net flow of aid resources in any given year. Particularly if the Government intends to ignore the 0.7% target as presently defined, and merely wishes to relate future aid to what it thinks Britain can afford, it would be more sensible for the annual readjustment to be applied to a more genuine net figure. (It was seen in Table 1.2 that in 1969-70 Britain's aid performance rating, compared to that of other DAC members, was not affected by deduction of interest as well as amortisation. Britain's interest receipts are projected[2] to drop from £29.3m in 1970 and £29.7m in 1972 to £26.8m in 1975: so long as Britain maintains a soft lending policy, therefore, deduction of interest would if anything probably tend, in the future, to show Britain in a favourable light relative to other donors.')

Private Investment

'Flows of private funds as well as official aid are expected to make a substantial contribution to the UNCTAD 1% target'[3]. The Government is following an active policy to stimulate additional private flows to developing countries; but before considering the detailed measures which have been proposed, we should refer to the rapid expansion of private flows which has already taken place in the last few years. The figures for the period 1965-1970, already shown in Table 2.1, are set out again in Table 3.2.

These figures serve to underline the importance of Pearson's reservations concerning the 1% target. In particular, they show that private

[1]See p.37.
[2]*British Aid Statistics* (1971), Tables 1 and 14.
[3]Cmnd. 4829, p.19.

flows fluctuate widely from one year to another (and it should be noted that flows to individual countries vary much more than the

Table 3.2   Private Flows from Britain to Developing Countries, 1965-1970

	1965	1966	1967	1968	1969	1970
Private Investment (net[1])	157·0	95·0	77·0	70·0	188·0	136·0
Export Credits (net[2])	38·3	47·1	41·3	58·1	110·8	181·8
Total (net)	195·3	142·1	118·3	128·1	298·8	317·8[3]

£m

Notes: 1. Net of disinvestment by UK residents or companies, but not of profit and dividend remittances.
2. Private export credits under official guarantee and with maturities in excess of one year. Net of capital repayments but not of interest.
3. The 1970 total shown in *British Aid Statistics* also includes, in accordance with the new DAC practice, grants by private voluntary agencies, estimated at £19m.
Source: *British Aid Statistics*, HMSO, 1970 and 1971.

global totals). The changing composition of the flows is also very noticeable : the net flow of export credits more than quadrupled between 1967 and 1970, so that in 1970 the volume of export credits (£181.8m) for the first time exceeded the volume of net private investment. In 1970, export credits constituted nearly 35% of the total flow of resources from Britain to developing countries.

It is sometimes suggested that export credits, compared to other private flows, make a less useful contribution to the development of recipient countries. Export credits do, however, enable the more effective exercise of local control over investment. Moreover, their financial cost – at least in terms of foreign exchange – can be precisely calculated; and there can be no doubt that some developing countries now prefer to use export credits rather than to accept new foreign equity investments.

As a corollary, an important feature of export credits, which distinguishes them from private direct investment, is that since the exporter – especially when he is able to obtain an official guarantee – has so much less at risk, greater responsibility, both for prior feasibility study and for subsequent efficient use of the equipment concerned, devolves on the importing country. It may be assumed that where the importer is a private firm, he is not likely to be negligent with regard to taking on repayment commitments which he will not be able to meet; and if his use of export credits is nevertheless contrary to the national interest, his government should – in theory – adjust its policies accordingly (for example, by reducing the level of tariff protection or by changing the country's exchange-rate).

Nevertheless, the growing use of export credits must also be a matter of concern – if not of worry – for the British Government. From the point of view of developed countries, export credits are essentially a means of promoting exports; and the insuring agency – in Britain, the Export Credits Guarantee Department (ECGD) – is primarily

48

concerned with assessing financial risks rather than with making a broader economic evaluation of particular investments. The Government does not make available any information concerning the distribution of export credits between different debtor countries (nor even concerning the total volume of repayment flows to Britain) and it may be asked whether some developing countries are being influenced – in their acceptance of additional medium-term liabilities – by the fact that developed countries, including Britain, have already shown that they are prepared to help out in extreme cases of unmanageable debt. All the credits listed in the official statistics have maturities in excess of one year; but, particularly if a significant proportion of them have maturities of less than, say, five years, the ECGD should at least read the recent increase in officially guaranteed credits as a danger signal. Increased use of export credits may, for a time, favour the rash rather than the deserving; but a few spectacular failures, such as have already been presaged by the debt crises in Ghana and Indonesia, could inflict real harm to the idea of partnership in development. It must be accepted that developing countries all too easily run into debt difficulties; and in Britain's case, the ECGD might be compelled to give closer scrutiny to insurance proposals if the Government made it clear that official development aid would not be diverted towards the refinancing of recipient countries' medium and short-term debts. Alternatively, if the credits now being extended are mainly concentrated in a relatively small group of 'safe' countries, it is all the more important to emphasise that for the developing world as a whole this category of finance is no substitute for official aid.

Contemporary discussion and debate about the prospective advantages and disadvantages which can accrue to a host developing country from other inflows of foreign private investment, is characterised by sweeping generalisations which at the present state of knowledge cannot be based on fact. Satisfactory conclusions can only be derived from a close examination of specific flows to particular countries (and comparison with corresponding outflows); detailed statistics are not made available; and, until recently, there had been very little research, even into the prospective economic and social effects of private direct investment alone. A joint team from Oxford and Sussex Universities has, for more than two years, been conducting an extensive investigation of the impact of private investment on the balance of payments, on real income and on employment, of host countries; and more fundamental research of this nature will be needed before it is possible to come to any general conclusions about, for example, the developmental value of different forms of investment. It is already clear, however, that although private investment may make a useful contribution to development, there are a number of functions carried out by official aid which it cannot perform. There are many needs – finance for social infrastructure and for peasant-based agricultural development, for example – which only official aid can meet; and quite apart from its inability to meet the sectoral development needs of a particular country (a shortcoming which in theory might be overcome, by a strong government, through an appropriate redistribution policy), it must also be emphasised that, in the nature of things, private investment is primarily attracted to those countries which offer the most promising commercial opportunities. These are *not* necessarily the countries which have the greatest need of development finance.

There is, admittedly, tautologous truth in the statement, contained in the Government White Paper[1] on British private investment in developing countries, that, 'Given the right conditions, private investment can benefit Britain and the host country at the same time'. Unfortunately, however, the White Paper does not provide a satisfactory definition of what these conditions are. It is not enough merely to say (as the White Paper does), that, 'The rapidly growing economies of some of the developing countries present favourable opportunities for private investment', but that, 'It is quite clear that no measures by us to stimulate the flow will meet with success unless the developing countries themselves are ready to welcome overseas investment'. Traditional foreign direct investment is a way of doing business which involves foreign control of the host country's assets : and there is growing evidence that such investment is becoming increasingly unattractive to developing countries, many of which have relatively undeveloped locally-owned private sectors. (In this connection, it should be observed that many developing countries, particularly in Africa, would question the White Paper's contention that they benefit from British private investment because it brings with it 'a general stimulus to local private enterprise'.)

In the present climate, any developed country government which seeks to encourage private investment in developing countries, and which is at the same time genuinely concerned that such investment should make a useful and widespread contribution to development, should try to identify forms of investment which are more acceptable to developing country governments. These broader questions will be discussed further below; but first we should outline the White Paper's proposals.

The most important of the new measures is the scheme for insuring new overseas investments against non-commercial risks. By 1971, Britain was almost alone among OECD industrialised countries in not having a Government-supported investment insurance scheme; and the British scheme, for which legislation was introduced in January 1972, is to provide cover against all the main types of political

[1]*British Private Investment in Developing Countries,* Cmnd. 4656, HMSO, April 1971.

risks (i.e. expropriation by the host foreign government, damage to property as a result of war or local disturbance, and inability to remit profits or repatriate the original investment). It will be administered by ECGD, which will have discretion to refuse or modify cover in particular countries or cases; and it is intended that the rates of premium, which initially will be based on the experience of other countries which have operated similar schemes, will be sufficient for the scheme to pay its way, taking one year with another.

The Government has also indicated in the White Paper that it hopes, wherever possible, to sign bilateral agreements with developing countries for the protection of new and existing investment. With regard to taxation, the Government has explicitly rejected any form of discrimination which would favour investments taking place in developing countries rather than elsewhere. The general conditions governing the giving of relief for foreign tax on the profits of a foreign company paying dividends to a British company are being relaxed slightly[1]; but there continues to be a degree of discrimination against all overseas investment, when compared to domestic investment in Britain.

Finally, the White Paper lists five ways in which the Government intends to use official aid in order to encourage private investment:

i) by forming more joint ventures between CDC and British private firms;

ii) by providing capital aid to host country development corporations, for use in partnership with British private capital;

iii) by offering, in order to encourage British firms to undertake pre-investment studies, to reimburse up to half the final costs of any study which results in the firm concerned deciding *not* to invest;

iv) by providing, on a normal government-to-government basis and therefore subject to local government request, aid for basic infrastructure associated with particular British private investment projects; and

v) by providing increased technical assistance in technical training in order to build up pools of skilled local labour.

With regard to most of these proposals, it will be virtually impossible to identify their individual or combined effect in stimulating additional investment flows. Some, particularly those concerning pre-investment studies and technical assistance, are essentially long-term in nature

[1]At present relief is due on any holding giving at least 10% voting control of a company in a Commonwealth country or in any other country where a double taxation agreement so provides; but outside these countries the British company must hold at least 25% voting control to obtain relief. The Government proposes to extend the lower 10% limit 'more widely'.

and indirect in impact; and others, particularly the signing of investment protection agreements and the more direct uses of aid to promote British investment, will partly depend on local government response. All in all, it can be assumed that the measures will have some positive effect in stimulating additional investment; but even the investment insurance scheme, which has the greatest potential for an immediate, widespread impact, will probably have only a very marginal effect on total flows, mainly by making it slightly more attractive to invest in countries which present reasonable commercial opportunities but relatively uncertain political prospects.

The conscious attempt to associate British aid with British foreign investment may be represented as a major step in the formulation of a comprehensive development policy. There must, however, be doubts about the nature of the policy 'package' which is emerging. It has already been suggested that in the present climate of opinion such a move may be diplomatically short-sighted. More important, the White Paper manifests an attitude, both towards private investment and towards the use of official aid to support such investment, which needs to be backed by more thorough social and economic evaluation. Official development aid should only be diverted to the support of British private investment if it can reasonably be assumed that this is desirable on developmental grounds. This implies considering all the other allocations, and especially other countries and other sectors. Such consideration may indeed indicate that the developmental value of aid is enhanced as a result of linking it to British private investment, but each case requires to be thoroughly and impartially appraised. One additional possibility, of which the Government should be aware, is that the main effect of subscribing capital aid to host country development corporations for use in partnership with British private capital, may merely be to reduce the amount subscribed by the British private investor. In such a case (i.e. where the private investor would have been willing to increase his subscription if forced to do so), the total inflow of capital resources would not be affected (but the British aid would at least enable greater control to be exercised over the project by the host country government).

Even where the British initiatives are welcomed by developing country governments, they may inhibit the adoption of an independent development strategy – one less dominated by Western thinking – such as Guy Hunter advocates in Chapter 7. Where they are not welcomed, Britain – together with other industrialised countries – should be sensitive to local political sentiment, appreciating that foreign investment is more easily accommodated – with less social upheaval and less potentially adverse polarising effects – in countries which have strong locally-controlled economies of their own. One of the Select Committee's recommendations is apposite :

'The growth of joint ventures with flexible arrangements for partnership and gradual agreed transfer of ownership and management should be encouraged.'[1]

Despite the Government's stated intention of promoting British private investment in partnership with CDC and with local development corporations, the importance of 'flexible arrangements for gradual agreed transfer of ownership and management' may be overlooked. The underlying philosophy needs, perhaps, to be re-oriented : so that Western countries look on their investments in developing countries more as leasehold, rather than freehold property.

Trade

The value of British trade with developing countries continues to rise, but more slowly than British trade with the world as a whole. The proportion of British imports supplied by developing countries fell from 33% in 1960 to 24% in 1970, and the proportion of British exports marketed in developing countries fell, over the same period, from 33% to 23%.

Thus, while continuing to be heavily dependent on supplies from developing countries of certain foodstuffs and raw materials, particularly oil, Britain is progressively re-orienting its trading pattern towards a greater emphasis on trade with other rich countries. British entry into the Common Market will accelerate this trend, with potentially adverse consequences for the trading prospects of some developing countries : this important issue is the subject of a separate chapter[2], and the present section, therefore, merely outlines four other policy issues which have a more immediate bearing on British trade with developing countries. These are the introduction of the British general preference scheme, the new cotton textile tariff, the relaxation of the rules which required imports into Britain to be marked with their country of origin, and the re-negotiation of the Commonwealth Sugar Agreement.

The general preference scheme is described at greater length in Chapters 1 and 6[3], but its recent implementation (in January 1972), since it recognises such an important matter of principle, must also be mentioned here. For the first time, Britain, together with seventeen other rich countries, is allowing duty-free or preferential access to a wide range of industrial and processed agricultural goods produced by developing countries, and is asking no corresponding preferential treatment in return. Importers and consumers in rich countries do, of course, stand to benefit from lower prices; and the immediate advantage

[1] HC (1970-71) 299, para 167.
[2] See p.92.
[3] See pp.16 and 108.

accruing to most developing countries, from any of the schemes, will be relatively small. Moreover, the British scheme, like most of the others, is thoroughly safeguarded with escape clauses. It will, in any case, need to be brought into line with the EEC scheme and the benefits to developing countries will be further diminished by the effects of increased competition, from the enlarged EEC, for the British market. Nevertheless, the very existence of the scheme represents an acknowledgement by the Government that trade preferences are a useful and proper means of favouring weaker countries (in a way which could, in small degree, serve to promote a more economic allocation of productive resources within Britain): and it should also be noted both that the Government played an important and constructive part in the international negotiations which preceded the schemes' introduction and that, if other countries had given equal support, a multilateral scheme – or at least a collection of rather more favourable bilateral schemes – might have emerged.

On the other hand, at least some of the benefit to developing countries from the British general preference scheme, may be offset by Britain's new cotton textile tariff. (Cotton textiles are specifically excluded from the preference scheme.) Up to the end of 1971, British cotton textile imports from developing countries were mainly controlled by a quota system, except that goods imported from non-Commonwealth countries were also subject to import duties. Since January 1972, import duties (amounting to 85% of the corresponding levies on imports from non-Commonwealth countries) have also been applied to goods originating within the Commonwealth; and although the Government had originally intended that these would replace the quota system, the previous quota restrictions have been maintained. India and Hong Kong thus continue to have relatively large bilateral country quotas; and for other developing countries there is a 'global' quota of which half is divided into 34 individual country quotas and the remainder is allocated, on a free competition basis, to British importers (who are free to import from any developing country, irrespective of whether it has a separate individual quota).

In retaining the quota, the Government is concerned to protect British textile producers. India and Hong Kong may also benefit from the continued protection which retention of their bilateral quotas will provide against increased competition from countries such as South Korea and Taiwan. The more competitive countries will certainly suffer, however. And although it is easy to understand the political motives for the Government's decision to increase protection, it is worrying – in terms of the long-term interests of Britain as well as of developing countries – that Britain, possessing a relatively inefficient and out-dated industry, should seek the easy way out, instead of making a more positive effort to restructure the domestic economy.

There is one other relatively small and unheralded change which, if it has any perceptible effects, will tend to encourage British imports (from rich as well as poor countries) of goods which we also produce ourselves. Since December 1971, Britain has abandoned the rules which previously required all imports to be marked with their country of origin. The effect of this change will be reduced by an amendment to the Trade Descriptions Act intended to prevent foreign goods from being marketed in Britain under British-sounding names. Nevertheless, the relaxation of the old rules will on balance tend to obviate consumer resistance to goods of unfamiliar origin; and although it may be that Japan will derive greater proportional benefit from the change than will, say, Brazil, some developing countries will almost certainly now find it easier to penetrate the British market.

Finally, and much the most important for a small group of developing countries, there is the Commonwealth Sugar Agreement. The long-term prospects for Commonwealth sugar are still in doubt[1]; but meanwhile, the Government has agreed to a substantial increase in the negotiated price. Since January 1972, the basic CSA price has been £50 a ton, compared to £43.50 previously; and the additional payments made to developing countries (and which vary according to the ruling world price) have been increased from between £1.50 and £4 a ton to between £7 and £11 a ton. The full price received by developing countries is now, therefore, between £57 and £61, as against £45 to £47.50 previously. The Government, still not certain how it will be able to honour its longer-term moral commitment towards the Commonwealth sugar producers, may have hoped, in agreeing to such a large increase, to gain short-term diplomatic advantage. The new price is still about £10 a ton lower than that paid by the EEC to France's Caribbean Departments, however; and it must be emphasised that whatever scale of increase had been agreed for the present interim period, this would not have absolved the Government from its responsibility to see that the producers' interests are safeguarded after 1974.

Towards an Integrated Policy

A properly based British development policy would be built on three main foundations, each of which would itself need to be based on wide-ranging and continually up-dated research. First, the Government would need to form a clearer picture of the problems now facing developing countries. (In this field there is of course no need for Britain to undertake independent research : it is much more desirable for Britain to play an active part in stimulating and co-operating in an international research effort.) Second, it would be necessary to forecast (albeit subject to controvertible assumptions) what particular mixture

[1] See p.107.

of policies would yield the greatest economic and social benefit to developing countries : this would require a more ambitious attempt to evaluate what British aid, trade and private investment policies are achieving at present. And finally, the Government would need to have a clearer view of what Britain is willing to afford, economically and socially, and would have to relate this to the cost of particular aid, trade or private investment policies.

It will be appreciated that none of these foundations could ever be securely laid : the ground can never be satisfactorily surveyed, and, like sand, it is continually shifting. Nevertheless, the Government requires to make a much greater effort to assess the short and medium-term cost of different policies. In particular, there seems to be virtually no attempt to fit trade policies into the picture. And concerning private investment, it often seems to be forgotten that British companies, where they invest in developing countries, do so because they judge that such investment will be to their advantage. It does not necessarily follow that private investment is of corresponding advantage to Britain (although this is generally presumed to be so); but, in any case, it needs to be emphasised that private investment policy could only be represented as 'aid' to the extent that it involves special concessions to developing countries, made with the purpose of contributing to their development and welfare. This could be done through a preferential tax policy, or through an insurance scheme which was *not* calculated to pay its own way; but the measures described earlier in this chapter are essentially catalysts rather than instruments of development assistance, and therefore (apart from the proposed use of British aid in support of British private investment) they cannot be described as 'aid'. It should, moreover, be repeated that the British aid effort should *not* be diverted to the support of British private investment, unless it can reasonably be assumed that the same aid could not be employed more usefully (for the developing countries) in other ways.

It would be naïve to pretend that development could always be the overriding priority in Britain's overall relations with the developing world. There will continue to be occasions when development policy is compromised in the interests of British political or commercial policy, and the Government will not always be able to publicise its reasons for acting in one way rather than in another. The fact remains that the Government should show itself more aware of the full developmental implications of its various policies : even in matters where developing countries are only indirectly affected, sound decision-taking can only be based on a more comprehensive attempt to identify what *development* requires.

PART II

4 United States Aid Performance and Development Policy

by James Howe and Robert Hunter[1]

Aid Performance

Recent trends in United States official development aid performance leave much to be desired, both absolutely and as a fraction of GNP. Although the flow of official development aid from the US is $3.1 billion, the largest in the world, it has actually declined since 1966 (see Table 4.2) both in monetary terms and much more in real terms.

Only one other DAC country has a similar trend. All others increased their official development aid.

Table 4.1   Recent Trends in US Resource Flows to Developing Countries: Net Disbursements, 1969-1970

	$m 1969	1970	% change
Official Flows			
Official Development Assistance[1]	3,163	3,119	− 1%
Other Official[2]	165	168	+ 2%
Total Official	3,328	3,287	− 1%
Private Flows[3]	1,459	2,155	+ 49%
Total Net Flows	4,787	5,442	+ 14%
Net Flows as a Percentage of Gross National Product			
Official Development Assistance	0·34	0·32	
Total Net flows	0·51	0·56	

Notes: 1. Consisting of aid administered by AID (see pp. 63 and 64), capital subscriptions to international institutions, agricultural commodity aid under Public Law 480, and the field costs of the Peace Corps.
2. Mainly consisting of Ex-Im Bank loans, and of Commodity Credit Corporation loans for sales of food.
3. Including reinvested earnings of $507m in 1969 and (estimated) $550m in 1970.
Source: *US Annual Aid Review for 1971*, Agency for International Development (AID).

Within the declining total of official development assistance, the US has increased both the proportion and the amount channelled through multilateral organisations. In September 1970 President Nixon proposed to the Congress that the US increasingly channel its development assistance through multilateral channels in the future. Action in the Congress during November 1971 also reflects support for contributions to international financial institutions. Nevertheless,

[1]James Howe and Robert Hunter are respectively Visiting Senior Fellow and Senior Fellow of the Overseas Development Council, Washington. The first four sections were written by James Howe and the final section by Robert Hunter.

Table 4.2 US Official Commitments and Disbursements, 1966-1970
$m

	Disbursements					Commitments				
	1966	1967	1968	1969	1970	1966	1967	1968	1969	1970
Official Development Assistance										
Bilateral										
Grants	1,452	1,480	1,313	1,360	1,393	1,713	1,656	1,457	1,522	1,499
Grant-like	977	843	633	442	320	827	744	218	240	192
Loans	1,286	1,319	1,386	1,383	1,397	1,464	1,513	1,862	1,000	1,213
Total	3,715	3,643	3,332	3,185	3,110	4,004	3,913	3,540	2,762	2,903
Multilateral	-24	310	252	330	393	495	694	444	608	507
Gross Total	3,691	3,953	3,584	3,515	3,503	4,499	4,607	3,984	3,370	3,410
Amortisation	61	81	66	96	121	—	—	—	—	—
Grant and Grant-like Recoveries	171	304	215	256	263	—	—	—	—	—
Net Total	3,459	3,563	3,303	3,163	3,119	—	—	—	—	—
Other Official Flows										
Bilateral Loans	406	487	701	609	732	492	943	804	592	779
Amortisation	341	332	397	444	564¹	—	—	—	—	—
Net Total	65	155	304	165	168	—	—	—	—	—
Total Official Flows										
Gross	4,097	4,440	4,285	4,124	4,235	4,991	5,550	4,788	3,962	4,189
Amortisation and Recoveries	573	717	678	796	948	—	—	—	—	—
Net	3,524	3,723	3,607	3,328	3,287	—	—	—	—	—

Note: 1. Includes $31m of outstanding indebtedness to Germany.

Source: Office of Business Economics, US Department of Commerce, 14 May 1971.

58

some opposition developed in the House of Representatives, over the shift from bilateral to multilateral assistance, on the grounds that the US should not lose control over its contribution to development assistance. In the Senate, meanwhile, some sentiment developed for an immediate phase out of bilateral aid. However, the speed with which the phase-over can take place is limited by the willingness of other donors to match an increased US contribution to multilateral bodies. Otherwise the US percentage of total contributions to any given body could get undesirably high.

The average geographical distribution of total official flows to developing countries in 1968-70 is shown in Table 4.3.

Table 4.3 Regional Distribution of US Net Official Bilateral Flows, 1968-1970 (Average)

	$m	%
Latin America	639	21·2
India and Pakistan	702	23·3
Other Asia	1,156	38·4
Africa	276	9·2
Oceania	45	1·5
Europe	92	3·1
Unallocated	100	3·3
Total	3,010	100·0

Source: *DAC Review 1971*, Statistical Tables 17 and 18.

Tables 4.4 and 4.5 show the current terms under which American aid is provided. The grant element of US official development assistance is running at about 65%, slightly lower than the DAC target of 70%. Otherwise the US terms generally meet the DAC tests for terms

Table 4.4 Terms of US Official Commitments, 1969 and 1970

$m	1969	1970
Official Development Assistance		
Grants	2,370	2,191
Loans	1,000	1,195
Total	3,370	3,386
Grants as % of Total ODA	70%	65%
Other Official Commitments[1]	592	740
Total Official Commitments	3,962	4,126
Grants as % of Total Commitments	60%	53%

Note: 1. All loans.
Source: *US Annual Aid Review for 1971*, AID.

Table 4.5 Average Terms of US Loans, by Agency, 1969 and 1970

	Maturity		Interest		Grace Period	
	1969	1970	1969	1970	1969	1970
Official Development Assistance						
AID	38·9	..	2·6	..	9·9	..
Public Law 480	31·5	..	2·7	..	7·8	..
Total ODA	35·0	36·0	2·7	2·7	8·7	8·9
Other Official Loans						
Ex-Im Bank	12·6	..	6·0	..	4·3	..
Commodity Credit Corporation	2·5	..	6·3	..	1·0	..
Total Official Loans	26·0	..	3·9	..	6·9	..

.. Not available.
Source: *US Annual Aid Review for 1971*, AID.

of aid. It may be that a US shift from bilateral to multilateral aid will increase the proportion of grants.

In May 1970, the United States indicated that it would join with other countries in untying bilateral assistance. In spite of the fact that this assurance was twice repeated in official US statements, the US, under pressure of severe balance of payments problems, has recently informed the DAC of its desire to postpone further negotiations on untying.

In early 1971, the US told DAC it expected that, over the next few years, multilateral development aid will rise, bilateral development aid will rise moderately and bilateral Food for Peace aid will remain relatively constant. Given further deterioration in Congressional support for development assistance, there is reason for scepticism towards these projections.

Aid Administration

The principal US development aid agency is the Agency for International Development (AID). It administers both a development loan and a technical assistance programme. On 15 September 1970 the President sent a message to Congress proposing basic changes in the administration of development assistance. He proposed :

1   To separate US military aid from US development assistance in the basic legislation.
2   To phase development aid gradually from bilateral to multilateral administration.
3   To separate development loans from technical assistance.

The Congress laid aside the President's proposals, pending further study. There appears to be some sentiment in favour of separating the legislation for military aid from that for development aid. As noted earlier, opposition has developed in the House of Representatives to the shift to multilateral institutions, though some Senators strongly favour it. Opposition has also developed to the proposal to split technical from capital aid.

Recently a new agency, the Overseas Private Investment Corporation, was created to administer the US insurance and investment guarantee programmes.

AID maintains offices in some 40 countries to help those countries formulate development projects and to monitor US aid programmes. AID has continued the trend begun some time ago of contracting with US universities and other private institutions and with other technical Government agencies to furnish needed technicians to developing countries. Fields of particular emphasis have included education, food production, nutrition and family planning.

In recent years AID has moved away from the practice of formulating comprehensive country development programmes. It has recognised that activities are most likely to succeed if they respond to programmes developed by the developing countries themselves.

Trade

The trend in US trade with the developing countries is shown in Table 4.6. It indicates that US trade with less developed countries (LDCs) has been growing steadily in the past ten years and that the US enjoys a substantial trade surplus with the LDCs.

Since before World War II, US policy has, for the most part, been to work towards a free trading system with a minimum of discrimination among trading partners. In 1962, the US took a new initiative in opening the so-called 'Kennedy Round' of negotiations to lower tariffs.

However, it was only near the end of the decade that the US announced its willingness to work for a system of generalised preferences for imports from less developed countries. President Nixon announced in early 1971 that he would submit legislative proposals to the Congress authorising the US to implement a generalised trade preference system; but to date (March 1972) no such legislation has been submitted. Many observers feel that the Nixon New Economic Policy (NEP) announced on 15 August 1971 has killed the chances for the US to honour its commitment to launch a generalised tariff preference scheme.

The NEP contained two elements potentially harmful to the developing countries. The first was an announced 10% cut in foreign aid. The cut was bad enough in itself. But observers feared that, together with the tone of economic nationalism in the New Economic Policy, it set the stage for irresponsible acts by the Congress: trade protectionism, deeper aid cuts, and a general rise of isolationism.

The second shadow cast by the NEP was the imposition of a flat 10% surcharge on many imports. The category of LDC exports hit hardest was industrial goods, their fastest growing sector and the one most beneficial to development. The surcharge was lifted in December 1971.

Other aspects of the NEP might be beneficial to the LDCs: (1) full employment in the US (if achieved) would increase US imports from LDCs; (2) exchange rate realignments stand to benefit some LDCs by making their exports more competitive in relation to those of Europe and Japan; and (3) partial replacement of gold and dollars by Special Drawing Rights (SDRs) could benefit LDCs if an increased share of new SDRs is distributed to them.

There is a wide measure of agreement in the US, both in and

Table 4.6 United States Trade with Developing Countries, 1960-1970

$m

	1960	1961	1962	1963	1964	1965	1966	1967	1968	1969	1970	Annual Growth Rate 1960-70
Exports to Latin America	3,550	3,490	3,280	3,240	3,770	3,730	4,170	4,080	4,660	4,807	5,648	4·7%
Imports from Latin America	3,600	3,270	3,300	3,380	3,400	3,530	3,890	3,770	4,060	4,214	4,779	2·8%
US Trade Surplus	-50	220	-20	-140	370	200	280	310	600	593	869	
Exports to Africa	490	610	780	730	840	770	920	730	790	861	987	7·2%
Imports from Africa	420	445	465	455	610	560	630	620	770	793	815	6·8%
US Trade Surplus	70	165	315	275	230	210	290	110	20	68	172	
Exports to Middle East	530	550	600	590	690	820	910	880	1,030	1,250	760	3·6%
Imports from Middle East	320	330	335	300	355	380	395	315	355	346	200	-4·8%
US Trade Surplus	210	225	265	290	335	440	515	565	675	904	560	
Exports to Asia	2,200	2,260	2,490	2,990	3,080	3,090	3,430	3,530	3,560	3,469	3,996	6·1%
Imports from Asia	1,190	1,200	1,210	1,280	1,440	1,660	1,780	2,040	2,420	3,040	3,402	11·1%
US Trade Surplus	1,010	1,060	1,280	1,710	1,640	1,430	1,650	1,490	1,140	429	594	
Total US Exports to LDCs	6,770	6,910	7,150	7,550	8,380	8,410	9,430	9,220	10,040	10,387	11,391	5·3%
Total US Imports from LDCs	5,530	5,245	5,310	5,415	5,805	6,130	6,695	6,745	7,605	8,393	9,196	5·2%
Total US Trade Surplus	1,240	1,665	1,840	2,135	2,575	2,280	2,735	2,475	2,435	1,994	2,195	

Source: Agency for International Development.

62

out of Government, that trade is extremely important to the development of the LDCs. About 75% of the foreign exchange available to LDCs comes from exports, compared with only 15% from aid and 10% from private capital. It is also clear that the rich countries benefited more from the negotiations completed in the Kennedy Round than did the poor countries. The LDCs' share of world trade is declining. Their imports cost more and their exports earn relatively less each year. Vigorous action is needed to give preference to their manufactures, to open rich country markets to their competitive primary materials, and to facilitate their trade with one another.

Private Flows

US private flows to LDCs during 1970 were about $2.2 billion, an increase of about $700m over 1969. This included increases in both direct and portfolio investment. As is shown in Table 4.7, US private investment is particularly important in Latin America. Virtually none of the increase occurred in Asia and Africa.

US policy on the export of capital generally favours the flow of capital to LDCs. The Foreign Direct Investment Programme, begun in 1968 to restrain capital exports, has rules which favour LDCs. And the incentive programmes of the new Overseas Private Investment Corporation include investment insurance : this guarantees US private investors in LDCs against certain hazards, including inconvertibility, expropriation, war, revolution and insurrection. In addition, OPIC subsidises the cost of pre-investment surveys. Finally, bonds placed by LDCs in US markets are exempt from certain US taxes.

Table 4.7   United States Private Capital Flows to Developing Countries, 1966 - 1970

	$m (preliminary) 1966	1967	1968	1969	1970
Direct Investment	656	790	1,248	750	1,060
(of which Latin America)	(308)	(296)	(677)	(344)	(555)
Other Long-term Capital	235	876	595	202	545
(of which: Latin America	(98)	(222)	(−45)	(45)	(152)
International Agencies)	(1)	(256)	(265)	(39)	(253)
Total excluding Reinvested Earnings	891	1,657	1,843	952	1,605
Reinvested Earnings	460	270	499	507	550
Total including Reinvested Earnings	1,351	1,827	2,342	1,459	2,155

Source : Office of Business Economics, US Department of Commerce.

United States Development Policy

This picture of reduced US aid flows to the developing world is not a pretty one. Even though the total volume of US aid is still larger than that of the next three largest contributors combined, our share must be seen in terms of our much greater wealth relative to these others. Nor is there much reason for optimism that the temporary defeat of the bilateral foreign aid programme by the US Senate in October 1971 will lead to a resurgence of support for this effort. In its present form, at least, economic aid is in for a lengthy time of serious trouble.

There were several short-term reasons for the Senate's action. Among other things, there was pique that many poor countries, as well as some rich ones, expressed glee at Taiwan's expulsion from the United Nations. There was the President's own 10% cut in foreign aid, announced on 15 August 1971 as part of the New Economic Policy, and his threat to veto the bill if it contained an amendment limiting US involvement in Vietnam. And there was a recognition that the vote would not really kill foreign aid, since *something* would happen in Congress to salvage most of it.

Yet these reasons were only surface appearances. Underneath, there has been a growing malaise surrounding the whole aid programme – a malaise that has been clear for some time.

To begin with, development aid has been caught up in the general revulsion in the United States against the war in Vietnam and the over-extension of US commitments during the 1950s and 1960s. The Cold War is over; and most Americans are simply tired of being told that they will be overwhelmed by 'things that go bump in the night' if they do not support open-ended efforts.

Economic development aid has been hit hardest by this new attitude – it is the bell-wether of US retrenchment. Except for aid programmes that generate US exports or votes for Congressmen – programmes like Food for Peace and aid to Israel – no one has been able to develop a political constituency for aid that carries much weight at the polls, in the campaign coffers, or in the lobbies of Congress. Similarly, the Administration is unwilling to commit any real political effort with a Congress controlled by the opposite party to salvage a sizeable economic development aid programme – even though it will still expend some effort in defence of foreign *military* aid and related economic programmes for security purposes, like the programme for Vietnam. Indeed, this continuing Presidential emphasis on military instruments of foreign policy has helped undercut support for military aid's economic twin sister – the weaker twin when the political chips are down on Capitol Hill.

In this regard, the aid effort in the US has to face more obstacles than similar efforts do under a parliamentary system of government. An Administration decision does not necessarily carry the day in Congress, and depends for its success partly on the President's placing his limited political capital behind development aid as opposed to other legislation he wants passed, perhaps in some totally unrelated field.

It was not surprising that liberal Senators, unable to work their will either on hastening US withdrawal from Vietnam or on curtailing military assistance for Indo-China on its own, took out their frustration on the entire foreign aid programme. Given the political forces described above, the result has been a further dwindling of economic development aid, while security programmes are still able to muster enough support, with strong White House lobbying, to satisfy Administration demands.

It may seem strange to outside observers that development and security aid ever became so closely intermeshed in the United States. But in context, the reason is obvious : economic aid has never been terribly popular in the United States except as an adjunct of some larger purpose of US foreign policy. For many years, it was seen by most people as a way of helping win the Cold War. Even the Marshall Plan, which set a record for popularity, was sold chiefly as a measure directly benefiting US national interests, and as an alternative to our one day sending large numbers of US forces to defend Europe. The element of altruism, though important to certain groups, was never dominant. Economic aid to the developing world has had a similar history : it has been accepted over the years by many supporters in Congress of US 'liberal interventionism' because it was deemed important as an adjunct of security policies whose primary focus was on military means. Thus the two programmes went through the Congress together; separately, it was feared by successive Administrations, economic aid would get nowhere.

In the shambles following the Senate's action last October, the reasons for continuing this practice disappeared also : it just will not work any longer. This may, however, prove to have been a salutary experience. The continued lumping together of all aid programmes is certainly not in line with the President's own recommendations to consider the security and development halves of the aid effort separately. It may even be possible in time to regain the term 'aid' for the field of development alone, as opposed to the blanket meaning it has today for all forms of foreign assistance.

Of course, it must be expected that an economic aid programme that has to go through Congress on its own will lose much of its support on the political right if it is no longer linked firmly to security programmes. But that could be a price worth paying, if in the process some way can now be found to begin building political support for economic efforts alone. Unfortunately, this is a big 'if'.

A change in nomenclature and of legislative tactics will not suffice to promote a major US role in development assistance. The rot is much too deep. Nor is development aid merely losing its support from the right; the left, too, is questioning whether it can actually achieve the many goals set for it. Liberals have argued, for example, that aid has not been a factor in keeping countries from 'going communist'; that it has not promoted democracy; that it does not buy influence; that it has not helped decrease the rich-poor gap, either within developing countries or as between them and us; and that far from providing 'stability', it rocks the boat.

There are certainly examples to substantiate each of these criticisms. Yet the problem lies even deeper : economic development aid should never have been *expected* to achieve these goals, except perhaps as a fortuitous accident. In the case of political goals, like containing communism, promoting democracy, or buying influence, the tools were usually inappropriate to the goals in question, even assuming the goals were valid ones; and with regard to questions of social justice within developing countries, in too many cases the quantities of aid were far too small, and the relationship of aid to development grossly exaggerated. The advocates of aid thus laid the groundwork for their own undoing : by promising that a limited instrument could achieve a host of collateral goals, they increased the chances that failure would be used to discredit even the legitimate purposes of aid. Ironically, this emphasis on collateral goals, in order to gain US political support for development assistance, also caused problems in poor countries that did not like being 'objects' of US foreign policy. The tension between two sets of rationales – for domestic and foreign consumption – led to further confusion in our way of looking at aid.

For all these reasons, therefore, the old coalition of forces on Capitol Hill that did manage to put through a development aid programme from year to year has broken apart. A new one will be long in building; and will suffer from the beginning from the lack of attention paid to the poor countries by Americans generally, and by Congress in particular. But even if attention can be gained, a new political coalition must be organised within a different intellectual framework – one that can appeal to Americans (and particularly legislators) who are inclined to ask 'Why bother?' when the issue of US relations with poor countries is raised.

To begin with, there needs to be a better understanding of the legitimate purposes of development aid, instead of those long claimed for it. These purposes can fairly be summarised as follows : to promote development to the extent that outside resources, skills, and ideas can supplement efforts by developing countries on their own. It is possible that there will be other achievements of aid. But it is important to realise that collateral benefits are just that, and that we have to be cautious in expecting them.

This proposition has to be part of a new intellectual framework supporting the politics of any major effort by the United States during the balance of this decade on behalf of economic development. It is not that the US should 'lower its sights' (that, after all, is simply an argument to reduce the quantity of development aid); it is rather that there has to be a restructuring of expectations, and willingness to accept

66

that the fruits of the effort may *not* fulfil any immediate purposes of a broader US foreign policy.

In the longer term, of course, there are things that countries *which are developing* may be able to do for us, provided that we get our attitude straight : development first, other benefits as a possible, if not certain, result. The US, after all, is finding with other nations that the developing countries will count for more than they have before as the world faces problems of a growing interdependence. The US has immediate needs to control traffic in narcotics; and there are broader questions of preserving environmental conditions that will make it possible for any nation, rich or poor, to survive and prosper.

So, too, there is currently under way a major restructuring of the international monetary system, which, to succeed, will require some co-operation from the poor countries. How much co-operation will be needed is not clear; yet the trend is firmly established. In addition, the growth and change of international trade will also involve rich-country, poor-country relations to an extent not hitherto known. This has become most obvious in shifting economic power in a number of basic commodities needed by the rich countries, beginning with oil. If the poor countries believe they are not served well by the existing system of international trade, therefore – or if there is continuing insensitivity in the developed world about the growing power of poor countries to bargain on some of these basic commodities – then both rich and poor will indeed suffer.

A case can be made that heading off these difficulties is a legitimate objective for the United States during the balance of this decade and into the next. Yet again, for the case to be a sound one, any progress made here must be represented as incidental to the development process. There is simply no guarantee that poor countries, as they develop, will be disposed to co-operate. Indeed, in some cases, development may lead to internal instabilities that will lessen, for a time, the chances of co-operation. And the success of development will likely only increase the ability of poor countries to exact a higher price from the rich for raw materials and products that we are accustomed to getting at bargain prices.

Despite this pessimism about the collateral benefits of development, it can be argued that *indifference* on the part of the rich countries to the needs and demands of the poor is even more likely to reduce the chances of gaining their co-operation on matters of interest to us. The same, of course, is true of the foreign investment that underpins a measure of our prosperity. The 'bum deal' given now may make amicable relations in the future much less possible.

This sense of the world's growing interdependence – and of the relationship of development assistance to the problems this interdependence is already posing – needs to be a basic tenet of any renewed political effort in the US to increase the flow of resources to the poor countries. It is not an air-tight, compelling case that could begin to rival the simple arguments of an indivisible Cold War in which allegiances have to be purchased in the interests of a global competition for power. Indeed, there are few *short-term* arguments that will carry much weight on Capitol Hill for development assistance, beyond the self-interest contained in the export-promotion element of development loans and the Food for Peace programme. It is also questionable whether any long-term arguments will soon generate much real enthusiasm among sceptical Congressmen and Senators.

None the less, these arguments for 'bothering' at least put the accent on the facts of trade, travel, investment, monetary co-operation, communications, environment, and transport that are coming to dominate the view that more and more nations have of the outside world and their relationship to it. And these arguments are also sufficiently broad to be made into a general philosophy about US relations with poor countries. Indeed, short-term emphasis on parochial interests like export promotion may be an enemy of the long-term, by not adding up to an attitude or approach that has any real coherence.

This emphasis on interdependence as a long-term trend also reinforces the widespread awareness in the United States that a new physical isolationism is no longer possible. But there is less awareness – and little understanding – of the possible consequences of a new isolationism in our attitudes. This is an indifference to facts as they are presented. In regard to our relations with poor countries, this indifference translates into an unwillingness to intensify the use of economic instruments of development assistance and to relate them to purposes that emphasise development first, rather than to collateral goals that can only be a by-product, if that.

Yet if this point can be got across, then it may be possible to gain attention for the fact that the record of development assistance is a more impressive one than the critics of today's programmes will attest. During the 1960s, for example, the poor countries did achieve the one real goal they set for themselves – namely, 5% growth. This was a remarkable achievement, that was unparalleled in the United States or in Europe during comparable periods of our own development. And the small facts of development – in roads, crops, disease-prevention, population control, water supplies, schools and transport – point to the efficacy of some effort.

These achievements need to be represented for their intrinsic value – and as goals to be pursued on their own in the first instance. Stress also needs to be laid on our need to exercise greater tolerance of mistakes and failures – a tolerance that is daily exercised in regard to domestic business and even some government programmes but which is muted when international 'charity' is in question. This will not be a simple or automatic process; ways will have to be found for changing the manner in which 'returns to investment' are viewed within a political system that most often deals in the very near-term; and there will have to be as much accent on matters of simple humanity as of long-term self-interest. But at least by viewing development assistance in this way, we have a chance to modify the old approach of measuring 'success' and to seek to build political support for efforts that are no more than they purport to be.

Of course, there will be challenge from a school of thought that opposes the diversion of funds from needed problems at home, or that does not accept a long-term definition of broader American interests in a world that *may* be more peaceful and promising (for ourselves as well as others) than would be the case in the absence of US concern and effort. Indeed, it is doubtful that the case for development assistance – or related issues, such as liberalisation of trade – will gain much currency until the US reduces domestic unemployment and achieves a more favourable balance of payments. This is more a problem of attitudes and self-preoccupation than of substantive challenge to programmes of development assistance.

But once these problems are met, there is a possible collateral goal in development that is worth considering with regard to the issue of broader US responsibilities. The theme of interdependence turns in part on a greater awareness of the role of economics in international politics, and of our new dependence on what other countries do in this area. This is an awareness that has still not permeated very deeply in the American Government, where there continues to be a preoccupation with military symbols and instruments of power. In relations between the US and the Soviet Union, for example, this concern is still a compelling one, even though it is somewhat less valid than it was even a decade ago. But with regard to other areas of US concern, more specific interests are involved.

This is particularly true in Asia, where at two ends economic factors are becoming of increasing importance. In India, sheer survival continues to be of considerable interest to the United States, as well as to a host of other countries that could not ignore the consequences of that country's going the way of Pakistan. Nor is this simply a humanitarian concern for one-seventh of the world's people. It is also a matter of continuing concern about the reach and motives of China, and of benefiting from the presence of a reasonably stable and developing India in the sub-continent and South-East Asian periphery. The key to India's being able both to survive and perhaps to play some kind of role in the area – however independent of other nations – is development. That much is clear. It also seems clear that outside help in the form of resources and technical assistance could make a significant difference.

The importance of economics may be seen also in the future role of Japan in East and South-East Asia. There, the Japanese are increasing their physical presence – through trade, aid and investment – by rapid stages. This is a development to be welcomed by the United States, as the best means both of postponing (and perhaps averting) a renewed emphasis on military rather than economic foreign policy in Japan, and of providing some 'presence' for the stable development of the region.

This in turn gives rise to a need for an American economic involvement – through trade, development aid and investment. These would not only contribute to the economic development of individual nations, but would also be particularly important as a buffering influence for Japan. Memories of World War II run deep in South-East Asia; and they are already raising anxieties about Japan's future role in countries like Thailand and Indonesia that also welcome the promise of economic advance that flows from Osaka. It is arguable, therefore, that a US economic involvement in the region is a necessary condition both for Japan's successful role in support of the ambitions of local states, and for helping to avert the emergence of dilemmas not unlike those that led us into Vietnam. Indeed, American *economic* involvement, coupled with that of Japan, holds the promise of replacing *military* involvements that have failed. The answer certainly does not lie in a military presence by another power after our withdrawal.

This kind of reasoning can be repeated elsewhere, particularly in regard to the US interest in retaining a place in the fast growing markets of the developing countries. In Africa, for example, US economic policy could help offset special preferential arrangements with the European Community that otherwise may effectively discriminate against goods coming from outside the region.

The central point is that there is new scope emerging for the use of economic instruments in US involvement abroad – and particularly the use of instruments that move resources to poor countries – that are both in support of objectives that will continue to be part of US concerns and will help countries in search of development. Furthermore, these instruments need to be employed now; the world will not wait for us to 'get our own house in order' first, whatever US domestic politics may dictate with regard to priorities.

Again, this US concern lies chiefly in the survival of countries in order to stave off the dilemmas that could be presented to the world by situations of chaos. US concern should not lie in types of regime, economic system, or voting habits at the UN. A missionary zeal on the part of the United States to create particular kinds of societies will be neither welcome nor effective. Rather, the US should be adopting a form of passive foreign policy; but it may none the less be in support of a kind of world that will be more congenial to the US as well as to others.

Even more important, it is clear that the United States *will* continue to be involved in many parts of the world. There can be no dismantling of all means for exercising responsibility. And even if such a course were possible, it would be most unlikely to take place, even if we (necessarily) restructure our 'world view' and (for a time) remain uncertain about the future of an outward-looking perspective that has developed here over the past thirty years, and is now in danger of some erosion.

The simple matter is that there *is* a Nixon Doctrine – i.e. a set of policies – that encompasses the developing world, and there will continue to be one. Again, there can be no US isolationism. So far, in addition to defining what the US will *not* do, this doctrine contains little of a positive nature that goes beyond efforts similar to the military assistance programmes of the 1950s. The question is whether this doctrine will evolve by design or by default. If the Nixon Doctrine is shaped by design, including major elements of economic development assistance, it is possible that development as a goal shared by the US and poor countries can become a major element of our outlook on the two-thirds of the world's people who are poor. But if the Nixon Doctrine evolves by default, and remains largely a set of military assistance programmes, we will have lost a rare opportunity to shift away from military means of expressing power and towards economic means of coping with a world of growing interdependence.

Provided we make the right choice, US 'national' objectives, such as having an intelligent Nixon Doctrine, can for once be reconciled with the objectives of poor nations that often see current US policies of trade and investment as being antithetical to their own growth and development. Claims made by poor countries for greater 'social justice' internationally may seem to strike at what the US wishes to protect today; but if we see that our best hope of 'protecting' a future in which we will continue to prosper requires us now to start taking the demands of the poor more seriously, we may be able to evolve an attitude, a foreign policy, and a set of relations with poor countries that will stand us in better stead for the future.

Even if it is possible to restructure attitudes towards foreign policy in this way – and to include heavy emphasis on development assistance as a *passive* instrument to promote development *for its own sake* – there will be major issues relating to method. It is clear that bilateral economic aid as we know it will have to be re-examined and altered. There are benefits to be gained from shifting the emphasis in lending to multilateral institutions like the World Bank – even though this will not eliminate all the dilemmas that exist in the donor-recipient relationship. Nor will there be support for this method from those Congressmen who favour bilateral administration of economic aid only because it does give us some control over how the money is used. There is also a need

71

to examine more closely non-appropriated ways of moving resources, including the use of SDRs and the resources of the sea-bed. And there is a need to revamp the machinery for administering what bilateral programmes remain, along lines suggested in the first section of this report.

But the essential point remains : that the United States can only maintain – and increase – its contribution to development if there is a radical recasting of the intellectual framework within which we view the developing countries and our relationship to them. This will not be a simple or rapid process. But it is probably the only one that offers any promise – however slight in the near future – for building a new base of political support for development assistance. This is not political support to salvage existing efforts by any means available, but rather to come to terms with America's place in the world during this decade and the next, and to fit within a new 'world view' a place for the developing countries that can be congenial to the interests of both them and us. Perhaps no such set of attitudes, principles and practices can be found. But that is no reason for not trying. The alternative, after all, is a compilation in future years of more dismal statistics like those with which this survey began.

5 Netherlands Aid Performance and Development Policy

by Dick van Geet

A Brief History of the Development Assistance Programme

The Dutch assistance programme has its origin entirely in post-war decisions. Although the Netherlands had in the past exerted control over vast territories in South-East Asia, the present-day Indonesia, there was no regular programme of official assistance in the current sense of the word. The turning point came shortly after the war when Indonesia became independent but the western part of New Guinea remained under Dutch sovereignty. This territory was not self-sufficient and required large amounts of assistance. Moreover, political considerations favoured the extension of a regular flow of aid, mainly provided in the form of subsidies covering the deficits of the local budget. Regular assistance was also provided to Surinam and the Netherlands Antilles. The first multilateral contributions were extended in the late 1940s in the framework of various United Nations programmes for technical assistance and relief.

In addition, some bilateral capital contributions were provided to third countries in the form of re-financing credits. These included a loan to Argentina in 1965 for the re-financing of private commercial debts. The first 'new' loan was extended, in 1959, to Turkey, in the framework of the OECD programme for the stabilisation of the Turkish economy.

The Netherlands' assistance programme during the past decade can be broadly classified into two periods, with 1963 as the dividing line. Until 1962, official net disbursements to less developed countries showed a steadily rising trend : from an annual average of about $17m during the period 1950-55 to $65m in 1962. Official bilateral aid, accounting for about two-thirds of the total, was almost completely concentrated on the Netherlands' overseas territories : more than 80% was extended in the form of grants, the bulk of which were budget subsidies to West New Guinea ($30.2m in 1962), and contributions to multilateral agencies rose from an annual average of about $1m during 1950-55 to $8m in 1957 and $25.5m (on account of an additional capital subscription payment to the IBRD and a first subscription payment to IDA) in 1961.

The year 1963 witnessed important changes not only in the volume, but also in the composition and direction of the Netherlands' assistance programme. As a result of the discontinuation of direct aid to West

73

New Guinea, which coincided with the final contribution to the first European Development Fund, net official bilateral disbursements fell from $46.7m in 1962 to $17.9m in 1963. Although contributions to UN agencies were stepped up, total contributions to multilateral agencies increased only moderately. Consequently, the net flow of official assistance dropped from $65.0m in 1962 to $37.8m in 1963.

As a result, the Government decided to expand the geographical scope of the aid programme through participation in consortia and consultative groups. The National Investment Bank was authorised by Parliament to lend for a provisional period of three years up to $13.8m annually under consortia and similar arrangements. The funds were to be provided out of the resources of the National Investment Bank and replenished by borrowing – with a Government guarantee – on the capital market. In addition, the Government decided to expand considerably its technical assistance expenditure, e.g. by organising a volunteer programme, a technical assistance project programme and a co-financing programme with private voluntary organisations.

Development Assistance Policies

The Netherlands Government regards its development assistance policies primarily as an instrument for the pursuit of peace. Its outlook may be summarised as follows. Recent history has clearly demonstrated the potential threat to peace which can arise from the existence of antagonistic blocks : there is now a real danger that the world might be split into two groups, the rich countries and the poor countries. It would be a catastrophic development if the present prosperity gap between the developed and developing countries were to result in permanent antagonism, in a form of international class-war; and every endeavour should be made to avoid such a polarisation.

In the first place, it is considered that rich countries, including the Netherlands, should assist in efforts to remove the basic cause of the tension – the Third World's poverty. Development funds must therefore be applied in such a way as to maximise their contribution to development, without any influence from the political or economic self-interest of donors. However, it is not enough just to concentrate on economic development. The greatest threats to peace do not always arise from purely material factors but more, perhaps, from pent-up emotion. Poor countries feel their inequality more deeply than in a merely economic sense; and in view of the long-term nature of the development problem, it is important that the development policies of rich countries should aim at removing and avoiding conflict by changing the atmosphere of contrast and antithesis into one of co-operation and mutual self-interest. Rich countries must therefore avoid anything which could stress the distinction between developed and developing countries, and instead must emphasise that all are partners

74

in one world-wide development effort which is equally important to both developed and developing countries.

It is for this reason that the Netherlands Government, in place of the term 'development assistance', prefers the term 'development co-operation'. Even this expression is perhaps felt to be inappropriate, because development is a process which largely takes place within the developing countries. It is the developing countries themselves which develop : the major responsibility lies with their own peoples and governments, and rich countries can only make a marginal contribution. Rich countries should commit themselves to providing assistance if and when they are requested to do so; and they should not seek, themselves, to guide the development process – on the grounds either that they are donors or that they have a greater understanding of the problem. They have to beware of trying to mould the developing world into an ideal image of their own design; and in order to avoid this sort of paternalism, the Dutch Government, as a matter of policy, leaves to recipient countries all decisions regarding the way in which its aid contributions are to be spent.

In pursuit of truly international co-operation towards peace, security and more equitable distribution of wealth, the Dutch Government attaches a very high priority to the International Strategy for the Second Development Decade, and considers this strategy as the main basis for its development assistance policies. The internationalism of the Strategy is felt to be a considerable step towards better mutual commitment and improved co-ordination; and the Netherlands has been a strong advocate of the Strategy's recognition of the need for better international division of labour, arguing that both developed and developing countries would benefit from it. Development co-operation involves participation of developed and developing countries on an equal basis, and it will bring about structural changes not only in the poor countries but in the entire world. The Dutch Government therefore acknowledges that developed countries must be equally prepared to accept such changes.

Co-operation in the Second Development Decade has made it necessary, at the national level, to enter into fixed commitments. Dutch development programmes are therefore now formulated in multi-year plans, and this requires long-term planning within the framework of the national budget. Dutch development assistance policy is also characterised by the channelling of a substantial share of the available funds through multilateral agencies or in the framework of international consortia and consultative groups.

Because the Netherlands realises that her total development contribution represents only just over 2% of the total flow of resources between donor and recipient countries, the available funds are concentrated, in the interests of efficiency, on a limited number of countries. In order to be considered eligible for selection, a country normally needs to have prepared a national development plan, and also to have a satisfactory past performance and to have shown willingness to co-operate in international co-ordinating arrangements.

Finally, the Government is concerned that a sober and realistic presentation of its policy should be given to the Dutch people. By stressing what rich and poor countries have in common, rather than the differences between them, the Government emphasises that development co-operation is a natural and useful instrument for the attainment of joint goals. Moreover, the Government seeks to work with appropriate private, groups in order both to identify the real nature of the development problem and to determine what specific contributions the Netherlands can make in pursuit of its development co-operation policies.

Aid Performance

Volume: Some Recent Trends

Since 1964, there has been a steady increase in the volume both of the total flow of resources and of official development assistance from the Netherlands to developing countries (see Table 5.1). With a small exception in 1967, the total flow of resources – both official and private – has since 1965 regularly exceeded 1% of the GNP. This is due both to a steadily expanding volume of official contributions and to a high level of private flows. The total flow of resources has almost doubled in the period 1965-70. The growth of official disbursements in this period averaged 25% per annum whereas the private flows increased by 7% per annum. Consequently, the share of official disbursements in the total flow has gone up from about 30% in 1965 to over 47% in 1970.

In 1970, official and private flows together amounted to 1.45% of GNP – or to 1.1% excluding oil investments – and official flows totalled $241.6m (compared to $175.5m in 1969): commitments of official development assistance amounted to $220.1m of which $21.5m was for re-financing operations.

The multilateral proportion in total disbursements has always been high when compared with the programmes of other donor countries. The Netherlands authorities have repeatedly stressed the importance they attach to this form of aid, which is considered conducive to an efficient use of resources while not involving the donor in setting up a costly administrative machinery. Thus disbursements of multilateral aid have been a notable feature in the overall programme. During 1964-67, they constituted between 32% and 47% of total official gross disbursements; but this share has somewhat decreased over the last few years, because of the rapid increase in bilateral aid.

The share of technical assistance expenditure in the overall programme grew rapidly between 1962 and 1966, from 2% to 29% of

76

Table 5.1 Total Net Flow of Resources from the Netherlands to Developing Countries, 1956 and 1960-1970[1]

US $m

	1956	1960	1961	1962	1963	1964	1965	1966	1967	1968	1969	1970
Official Development Assistance												
Bilateral												
Grants	21	26·1	31·7	42·4	9·9	13·1	14·6	22·0	43·3	54·9	68·4	93·5
Net Loans	16	−1·6	−1·3	4·3	8·0	19·9	32·2	27·2	32·2	44·1	39·1	61·1
Total	37	24·5	30·4	46·7	17·9	33·0	47·1	50·5	75·5	99·0	107·5	154·6
Multilateral	11	10·8	25·5	18·3	19·9	16·2	22·5	44·4	38·0	24·4	35·6	41·8
Total	48	35·3	55·9	65·0	37·8	49·2	69·6	93·9	113·5	123·3	143·1	196·4
Other Official Flows	—	—	—	—	—	—	—	—	—	11·1	6·7	18·6
Total Official Flows	48	35·3	55·9	65·0	37·8	49·2	69·6	93·9	113·5	134·4	149·8	215·0
Private Flows	232	203·3	144·4	49·2	96·6	69·2	169·2	160·2	114·7	141·1	219·4	240·6
Total Net Flows	280	238·6	200·3	144·2	134·4	118·4	238·8	254·1	228·2	275·5	369·2	455·6
Net Flows as a Percentage of Gross National Product												
Official Development Assistance	0·53	0·31	0·45	0·48	0·26	0·28	0·36	0·45	0·49	0·49	0·51	0·63
Total Net Flows	3·10	2·11	1·61	0·85	0·92	0·69	1·24	1·22	0·99	1·09	1·31	1·45

Notes: 1. Net of amortisation and disinvestment, but not of interest, profit and dividend remittances.
Sources: *Development Assistance Efforts and Policies of the Netherlands*, Ministry of Foreign Affairs, The Hague, 1968.
Explanatory memoranda to Development Assistance Budgets.
Development Assistance Reviews, OECD.

total official disbursements. However, in the last few years, technical assistance expenditures, too, have declined relative to total disbursements, representing 15% of the 1970 total. Expenditure on technical assistance is allocated between experts, volunteers, fellowships and projects. In addition, there is a technical co-operation programme with private voluntary organisations.

Geographical Distribution

A large part of bilateral assistance has always been directed to the Netherlands' overseas territories, i.e. the Netherlands Antilles and Surinam (see Table 5.2). The Netherlands' contributions to the funds required for the economic and social development plans of these territories has represented about 10% of the total national income of these countries, and in 1963/64 they accounted for more than 70% of total Dutch official bilateral assistance. In the last few years, there has been a downward movement in the relative share of aid to these territories; but this is due to the overall increase in development funds. Although the percentage share in the budget decreased from 22.2% in 1970 to 21.6% in 1971, there was in fact an increase from $48m to $58m. Such amounts represent a very high level of assistance per head : the total population of Surinam and the Netherlands Antilles together is barely 600,000.

Table 5.2 Netherlands Official Development Assistance: Disbursements, 1968-1970, and Budgetary Appropriations, 1969-1972

US $m

	Disbursements			Appropriations			
	1968	1969	1970	1969	1970	1971	1972[1]
Gross Bilateral							
Overseas Territories	34·6	33·1	49·5	42·2	48·2	58·0	62·8
(Grants)	(18·3)	(18·6)	(34·0)	..	..	(41·6)	..
(Loans)	(16·3)	(14·5)	(15·5)	..	..	(16·4)	..
Loans to Consortia and Consultative Group Countries[2]	26·3	20·2	43·5	27·7	47·1	58·7	
Indonesia (Capital Assistance Grants)	15·6	9·0	20·7	14·7	9·5	14·8	92·8
Technical Assistance	20·9	30·3	29·8	34·5	41·0	50·7	60·1
Other	3·7	13·2	13·8	19·2	32·2	36·2	23·8
Total	101·0	105·7	157·3	138·3	178·9	218·4	239·5
Gross Multilateral	26·5	38·3	41·8	39·8	34·6	45·7	50·6
Gross Total	127·5	144·0	199·1	178·2	213·6	264·1	290·1
Amortisation	4·2	1·0	2·7	..	..	..	..
Net Total[3]	123·3	143·0	196·4	..	..	..	..

Notes: 1. As presented to Parliament.   .. Not available.
        2. Including loans to Indonesia.
        3. Net of amortisation but not of interest.
Sources: Same as for Table 5.1.

In 1963 the Netherlands Government decided to widen the geographic scope of its capital assistance programme. It confined its choice of recipient countries to those for which the World Bank, the OECD or the IDB have organised consortia or consultative groups. Apart from these countries, no capital assistance is extended, except to the Netherlands overseas territories and Indonesia, and through multilateral channels. This policy decision recognised the difficulties, for a relatively

78

small donor, of selecting any particular recipient country for purely bilateral aid. It has led to a better co-ordination of Dutch assistance with that of other donors; and it has provided the benefit of a joint assessment of the influence of aid and of self-help measures on the development of recipient countries. Thus, bilateral financial assistance has since 1967 mainly been concentrated on nine countries – Indonesia, India, Pakistan, Kenya, Tanzania, Uganda, Tunisia, Colombia and Peru – and also, but not continuously, on Sudan, Nigeria and Turkey. Consideration is now being given, in view of the fast growth of budgetary appropriations, to the desirability of extending bilateral capital aid to a slightly larger number of countries.

An important event in 1965/66 was the resumption of capital aid to Indonesia, when the Indonesian Government urgently needed support for its efforts to cope with the serious economic situation. Since then, assistance to this country has increased every year. In 1970, of the total allocation of loans via consortia and consultative groups, amounting to $58.7m, more than $14m was earmarked for loans in the framework of the Inter-Governmental Group on Indonesia.

A special element in the bilateral financial assistance programme consists of loans to Latin America. In 1965 the Netherlands Government signed an agreement with the Inter-American Development Bank to finance development projects in Latin America in co-operation with the Bank, in order to benefit from the latter's expertise and thus assure efficient utilisation of aid funds. The loans extended under this scheme are the only type of capital assistance under the Netherlands programme which is clearly linked to specific projects. All other financial assistance is extended in the form of programme aid, i.e. general purpose contributions not related to identifiable projects.

Compared to capital aid, technical assistance has a much wider geographical distribution.

Terms

Dutch aid has always been extended on comparatively soft terms. In 1970 commitments for grants and grant-like flows amounted to about 64% of total commitments for official development assistance. Expressed as a percentage of GNP, commitments of grants have shown a continuous increase in the first three years of the first Four-Year Plan for development assistance, from 0.31% in 1968 to 0.37% in 1969 and 0.42% in 1970. With a few exceptions, loans are made on terms which conform with those advocated by DAC : at $2\frac{1}{2}$% interest and with repayment over 30 years including an 8-year grace period. Loans to Latin American countries have hitherto been extended on terms comparable to those charged by the IDB, i.e. about $6\frac{1}{2}$%. But they are now to be made at the same terms as the loans to other countries.

Procurement Policies

Though Dutch capital aid is formally untied, it is effectively tied almost completely – through a 'gentleman's agreement' whereby recipient countries have to procure goods to the largest possible extent in the Netherlands. The choice is, moreover, limited to a specific list of goods.

There is an exception for loans to Latin America, to the extent that only 80% of purchases have to be made in the Netherlands. The remaining 20% may be used, in appropriate cases, to finance local costs.

Future Policy and Projections
The increase in the aid budget from 1970 to 1971 amounts to about 24% (see Table 5.2): the largest in the Plan period 1968-1971. This increase was required in order to meet the Plan's target that total aid appropriations should equal 1% of national income at factor cost in the last year of the Plan period. (This budget target corresponds to about 0.7% of GNP at market prices : amortisation receipts will continue to be fairly low, and the UN 0.7% target for net official development assistance may therefore also be reached in 1972.) When the Plan was prepared, it was estimated that an appropriation of $229m would be sufficient to achieve the target, but this estimate has since proved too low because the national income in money terms has risen faster than was originally expected.

The Government has now presented to the Netherlands Parliament, as part of the explanatory notes to the Foreign Ministry's 1972 estimates, a second Four-Year Plan for co-operation with developing countries. The basis of the new Plan, which covers 1972-1975, is the Government's decision to allocate $1,400m for development co-operation during the whole period. This represents a 66% increase over the last Plan period; and the total is to be spread over the coming years as follows :

1972	$291.7m	(+8%)
1973	$319.4m	(+9%)
1974	$368.0m	(+15%)
1975	$423.6m	(+15%)

As in 1968, a long-term plan has been adopted in view of the long-term character of the development problem and the number of years over which development activities extend. The plan is indicative only, and both the policy and the distribution of funds envisaged in it may be revised in the light of new facts and ideas. Adjustments will be made at the time when the annual estimates are drawn up.

Co-operation with Private Voluntary Organisations
To stimulate development activities by private voluntary organisations the Government finances, on a grant basis, 75% of the capital outlay of approved projects. Most of these are in the social field, e.g. schools

and health centres, and the budgetary appropriations for the co-
financing of this type of project have doubled in the last few years.
The Government also subsidises a number of private institutes which
undertake research in the field of development assistance.

Aid Administration

The Netherlands' aid administration has been in continuous evolution.
As the programme expanded, more ministries became involved with
the execution of development policies, and eventually the need was
felt for inter-departmental co-ordination and administrative centrali-
sation. This led in 1963 to the appointment, within the Ministry of
Foreign Affairs, of a Secretary of State with special responsibility for
development assistance, and to the establishment of a new Directorate-
General for International Co-operation, also within the Ministry of
Foreign Affairs, in 1964. In the same year an Inter-Ministerial Co-
ordination Committee was set up; and in 1965, a Minister without
Portfolio was appointed, within the Foreign Ministry, with overall
responsibility for development policy. Further, in order to assist the
Government in drawing up its aid programmes, a National Advisory
Council was established in 1963. This consists of about 70 representa-
tives of various economic, social and cultural groups in the Nether-
lands, and it has produced a number of reports, at the request of the
Minister for Development Aid or on its own initiative.

The appointment of the Minister without Portfolio constituted an
important step towards administrative concentration, and has since had
the effect of putting the consideration of aid concepts and methods on
a more systematic and rational basis within the administrative bodies
concerned. The Minister also presides over the Inter-Departmental
Committee which co-ordinates the policies of the various ministries.
His main function is to direct, co-ordinate and promote the aid programme as a whole and, in the absence of a separate departmental
budget for development assistance, to present a detailed budgetary
statement to Parliament grouping together the requests for aid appropriations.

Various ministries and organisations are concerned with the different
types of aid extended. For example, the Foreign Ministry administers
the contributions to the United Nations agencies as well as the technical assistance programme. Aid to the Netherlands' overseas territories
is the responsibility of the Deputy Prime Minister's Office and the
Ministry of Finance. The Ministry of Economic Affairs is concerned
with the utilisation of loans extended under consortium and consultative group arrangements. The Ministry of Finance is concerned, among
others, with policy concerning aid terms; and it provides for interest
subsidies out of its budget. The Netherlands Investment Bank for
Developing Countries initially financed all Government guaranteed

development loans to consortium and consultative group countries, but since 1966 these loans have been financed out of the State Budget.

Trade

Since Dutch trade policy with developing countries is mainly an EEC matter, we will not consider it in much detail. The potential for Dutch action in this field is to a large extent limited to efforts within the Common Market to promote developing countries' exports. The Netherlands has argued in favour of an early implementation of the system of general trade preferences for developing countries; and mention should be made of the recent establishment in Rotterdam of a centre for the promotion of the sales of products of developing countries. Moreover, the Dutch Government continues to allow free exhibition space for developing countries at the annual Utrecht Trade Fair : in 1970 six developing countries made use of this facility. Funds were also made available for a symposium on export promotion organised by the UNCTAD/GATT International Trade Centre in Latin America. Support is given to the growth and diversification of developing countries' exports, and the Netherlands participates in international agreements for the stabilisation of the export prices of some raw materials, such as coffee and tin. As a new step in this field, the Netherlands has made a voluntary contribution to the financing of a buffer-stock under the Fourth International Tin Agreement.

An indication of the extent of Dutch trade with developing countries is given in Table 5.3.

Table 5.3 Netherlands Trade with Developing Countries[1], 1963-1966

	$m 1963	1964	1965	1966
Exports to Latin America	186	203	192	241
Imports from Latin America	303	307	310	296
Netherlands Trade Balance	−117	−104	−118	−55
Exports to Africa	171	179	211	214
Imports from Africa	252	300	308	322
Netherlands Trade Balance	−81	−121	−97	−108
Exports to Middle East	93	114	119	129
Imports from Middle East	342	371	365	389
Netherlands Trade Balance	−249	−257	−246	−260
Exports to Far East	154	176	199	200
Imports from Far East	119	204	213	207
Netherlands Trade Balance	+35	−28	−14	−7
Total Exports to LDCs	714	804	894	960
Total Imports from LDCs	1,064	1,246	1,267	1,290
Overall Trade Deficit	350	442	373	270
Exports to LDCs as % of Total Netherlands Exports	14·4%	13·8%	14·0%	14·2%
Imports from LDCs as % of Total Netherlands Imports	17·8%	17·7%	17·0%	16·1%

Note: 1. Excluding European countries.
Source: *Overall Trade by Countries*, OECD, July 1967.

Private Flows

The Netherlands has always been an important source of private capital for developing countries. In recent years the private flows of resources have usually exceeded, often substantially, the volume of official aid disbursements (see Table 5.1). Overall, there appears to be an upward trend in the total private flow, though the main components, especially export credits, tend to fluctuate from year to year (see Table 5.4).

Table 5.4 Netherlands Private Capital Flows to Developing Countries, 1965 and 1968-1970[1]

	$m 1965	1968	1969	1970
Direct Investment	108·6	89·9	165·9	211·7
of which: Petroleum	70·0	26·4	80·4	105·0
Other	38·6	63·5	85·5	106·7
Portfolio Investment	17·1	63·6	28·1	26·5
Export Credits	43·5	−11·8	25·4	2·4
Total[2]	169·2	141·1	219·4	240·6

Notes: 1. Net of capital repayments and disinvestment, but not of interest and dividends.
2. Excluding grants by private voluntary agencies ($5.2m in 1970).
Source: DAC Reviews and official Dutch publications.

Netherlands direct investment in developing countries is dominated by four firms: Royal Dutch, Unilever, Philips and AKZO. The two largest companies – Royal Dutch and Unilever – are jointly owned by Dutch and British shareholding interests.

Private export credits are eligible for Government guarantees. The N.V. Export-Financierings-Maatschappij (EFM) is the most important export credit financing institution. 60% of EFM stock is held by the National Investment Bank of the Netherlands and 40% by various commercial banks, and EFM's resources consist mainly of loans raised on the capital market. Almost all export credits extended to developing countries are guaranteed by the 'Nederlandse Credietverzekering Maatschappij N.V.'.

In 1967 the Government introduced a scheme for the insurance of investments in developing countries against political risks. As far as commercial risks are concerned, in 1966 a form of co-operation with private business was established whereby the Dutch Government could take over up to about 50% of the economic risks of 'starter projects' – the initial investments made by private medium-sized firms in any particular developing country. Up to May 1970, total public assistance for these starter projects amounted to $6.2m, and this had generated $19.2m of private investment.

Most activities for the promotion of private investment in developing countries were brought together in 1970 with the establishment of the Netherlands Finance Company for Developing Countries (FMO), a joint venture between the Dutch Government and private business. To a fairly large extent, FMO's goals and activities are comparable to those of Britain's Commonwealth Development Corporation, though it should be observed that there seems to be much less interest in Dutch business circles for the FMO than exists in Britain for the CDC.

Some Comments on the Aid Policy and Performance of the Netherlands

It was stated earlier that Dutch aid policies are viewed as an instrument for the pursuit of peace and the avoidance of a polarisation between developed and developing countries. Rich and poor countries were seen as partners in a world-wide process of development, and aid policies were to be in harmony with this basic idea. In the context of this philosophy, Dutch policies were outlined. Subsequently, the facts and figures of Dutch aid performance were presented. It is now possible to consider the extent to which practice accords with policy.

One element of Dutch aid policy appears to be the desire to avoid paternalism, with its attendant conflicts, and consequently to allow developing countries to determine how the aid received should be spent (page 79). Yet this is somewhat difficult to reconcile with the Dutch procurement policy (page 83), which often involves double-tying of aid. In practice, then, developing countries have only a limited control over the utilisation of Dutch aid.

The criteria for the allocation of aid to a limited number of countries are said to be based on the development performance of those countries and their willingness to co-operate with international co-ordinating arrangements, such as consortia and consultative groups. Even allowing that these criteria are consistent with the overall goal – that aid should be an instrument of peace – there are some points which require clarification. At least 20% of Dutch aid has been directed towards the Netherlands Antilles and Surinam (page 82). It would seem likely that this volume of aid was determined more by these countries' historical and commercial links with the Netherlands than by the above criteria – or indeed by the pursuit of peace. Secondly, the choice of the countries of concentration for Dutch financial aid, other than those countries associated with the Netherlands by historical links, appears to be as much determined by a desire for an adequate geographical representation of politically acceptable recipients, as by the specified criteria.

The criteria themselves should be considered. Certainly, for the sake of efficiency, it makes sense to direct aid towards those countries which have shown willingness to participate in international co-ordinating arrangements. However, there are undoubtedly countries which are willing but not able to co-operate with such groups for the simple reason that they do not exist – and are thus ineligible. One may question the desirability of limiting the scope of Dutch aid in this way.

Turning to the allocation of aid to multilateral agencies, a further discrepancy may be observed. While the proportion of multilateral aid in Dutch disbursements has always been relatively high compared with that of other donors (page 80), the amount is less impressive when set against the background of the Dutch policy aims of promoting international co-operation, harmony and peace in the context of the International Strategy. The fact that the bulk of aid is still bilateral and tied, suggests that there are other, less high-minded, purposes – such as the pursuance of Dutch commercial interests.

Concerning the volume of aid, the Dutch budget target of 1% of net national income (about 0.7% of GNP) has almost been achieved (page 84). However, this provides a misleading impression of the actual aid flow. First, the 1% target (which should not be confused with the UN target for *total* flows to developing countries) was reached with the help of some statistical juggling whereby items, hitherto excluded, were brought into the budget. Secondly, the budget includes items which can only be dubiously categorised as development assistance: for instance, the financing through the Netherlands Finance Company of measures to encourage Dutch foreign private investment (page 87). Even supposing that these measures are in the interests of developing countries, the private investor will not generally be motivated by a desire to help the developing country. Finally, the aid budget is expressed in gross terms and thus does not take account of return flows of amortisation and interest payments. Amortisation receipts are still relatively low. On the other hand, roughly one-third of new Dutch official development assistance consists of loans. Although these are extended on fairly soft terms (page 83), it is therefore clear that, so far as pure assistance is concerned, the Government's 1% target has not yet been realised. Nor will it be realised in the near future. (Similar criticisms may be applied to other countries' aid programmes: the real aid performance of all donor countries would be much clearer if all return payments, including interest, were subtracted from the gross flows or if aid was expressed in terms of the grant element of amounts disbursed.)

In the field of trade, there is considerable potential for reducing the dangers of a polarisation of the world into two hostile blocks of rich and poor countries. In the international context, for instance at UNCTAD, the Netherlands has the opportunity to make efforts to move towards greater co-operation between the two groups. However, although the Netherlands is relatively progressive, trade policies do not conform with the stated government policy aims towards the developing world. Such conformity has been inhibited by the fact that policy vis-à-vis UNCTAD has been the responsibility of the Minister of Economic Affairs, whose concern is primarily with the trading problems of the Netherlands rather than with those of developing countries. Further, although the Netherlands acknowledges the need to bring about structural changes in the domestic economy to facilitate trade liberalisation and a more efficient international division of labour, in practice little is done. A few very inefficient industries may be allowed to disappear; but, on the whole, the Netherlands is prepared to shelter behind the protection provided in the general framework of EEC policy – even when goods are produced relatively more efficiently in LDCs.

Finally, it was seen that it is the intention of the Government that the Dutch people be given a sober and realistic presentation of its aid policy. The presentation given is perhaps sober. Whether it is realistic is open to question, given that the points raised above are rarely mentioned.

Overall, it is possible to conclude that there are considerable discrepancies between official philosophy and actual practice. But these cannot merely be ascribed to hypocrisy: to a large extent, they stem rather from the domestic political situation and from the way in which aid administration has evolved.

The official aid policy originates from the sphere of the Directorate-General for International Co-operation, which has a co-ordinating position as far as development assistance is concerned. This basic philosophy is shared by the Minister without Portfolio, and by those who are directly concerned with aid. Policies are thus determined in the interests of developing countries and as such are laudable. The problem arises in that the instruments for implementing these policies are inadequate to the task.

Almost a quarter of development assistance (to Surinam and Netherlands Antilles) is in fact outside the sphere of responsibility of the Minister without Portfolio. For the rest, aid policy is subject to the conflicting interests of the different ministries responsible for implementation: ministries which represent Dutch interests rather than those of LDCs. Thus, the tying of Dutch aid is to a large extent influenced by the Ministry of Economic Affairs, and the terms and conditions of aid by the Treasury. Further, the very fact that the Minister for Development Aid is operationally attached to the Ministry of Foreign Affairs means that development aid runs the risk of being used as an instrument of short-term foreign policy. Moreover, it may be argued that the grafting of aid administration on to this Ministry, with its older and perhaps somewhat rigid structure, has led to some dissipation of the idealism and dynamism of the aid administration.

Dutch aid performance, compared to that of other donors, is reasonably good. The aid *policy* itself might even be called far-sighted in its conception of the problems which will face the world in the future. It is, however, clear that Dutch domestic interests influence its implementation and that much that comes under the heading of development assistance only deserves this name in a very limited sense. There is a need to separate out those activities performed specifically in the interests of developing countries, from those activities which may be related to developing countries but are not primarily motivated by a desire to assist their development. Only the former should be designated as development assistance. Such a division can only come about if the responsibility for aid policy and administration is confined to those charged solely with the interests of the developing countries.

If the view that no one can serve two masters were to be wholeheartedly adopted by Dutch policy-makers, especially the aid administration, the future prospects for Dutch aid performance might improve considerably. Fortunately, a section of Dutch public opinion does support the interests of the developing world and is resentful when development funds are used to serve other ends. However, their criticism is often directed, mistakenly, at those who are genuinely trying to serve the interests of the developing world, but are only partly able to do so because of the influence of conflicting vested interests.

6 Developing Countries and the Enlargement of the EEC

by Peter Tulloch

For Britain, the 'Great Debate' on the principle of entry to the EEC ended with the Parliamentary vote in October 1971 and the signing of the treaty of accession in January 1972. At this point, therefore, the emphasis of the debate should alter from discussing the merits or demerits of British entry to the Community to determining what kind of a body it is that Britain is joining and discussing the directions in which Britain, as a major member of a Community of ten, ought to exert its influence in policy-making.

It is quite clear that the relationship between an enlarged Community and LDCs is not a marginal matter. A few figures will suffice to illustrate the point. 30% ($2,013m) of net official development assistance from DAC members in 1970 derived from the 'Six' and 38% from the 'Ten'[1]. Moreover, the 'Ten' together purchase over 40% of total exports from LDCs. Their economic influence for good or ill is, therefore, considerable.

This chapter aims to identify and clarify some of the main problems which may be faced by developing countries as a result of EEC enlargement. There are three main areas of policy which give rise to immediate apprehension. First, the influence of the concept of association with the Community on relations with LDCs in general and in particular with those which are not currently seen as potential associates. Second, the effects of Community agricultural policies on world and, in particular, LDC trade in farm products. And, finally, the effects of the General Preference scheme as applied by an enlarged Community. In the longer run, broader questions are raised concerning the policies of the Community as a group, and of member countries individually, towards developing countries.

There is no obvious economic rationale underlying the existing *de facto* division of responsibilities between the Community and the member states. The Community deals with tariff policy and hence preferences, as well as with matters covered by Conventions of Association – including a small amount of aid through the European Development Fund (EDF). Most aid is negotiated and spent bilaterally, however, while policies governing overseas investment, some areas of external commercial policy, as well as overall political relationships, are determined by national governments. This raises several questions. First, how far should an attempt be made, in a trade and aid group as big as the enlarged ten-member EEC, to bring all such

[1]The Six plus Britain, Eire, Denmark and Norway.

88

policies under Community responsibility? Second, if this were to be achieved, should the enlarged Community's policies towards LDCs be based on the present 'regional' concept of association, which derives in part at least from relations created in colonial history, or rather on a broader global view of trade and development? And lastly, if the latter view were taken, could the existing 'European' aid channels (the EDF and the European Investment Bank) form an apposite framework for Community aid disbursement on a much larger scale, or would the interests of LDCs be better served if these funds were channelled through truly multilateral organisations like the World Bank? Community enlargement – and in particular the entry of Britain, with its historically different view of the developing world to that of the Six – provides the opportunity needed for a general review of such policies.

Association with the Community

In the immediate future, the degree to which Britain's freedom of action on broad questions of aid and foreign investment will be maintained depends, very largely, on the number and importance of the Commonwealth LDCs which choose to become associates, and on the type of association agreement which they choose. Under the negotiated agreement between Britain and the EEC, British dependencies (except Hong Kong and Gibraltar) are offered association with the enlarged Community under Part IV of the Treaty of Rome; to be negotiated by 1974 when the Yaoundé association convention is renewed. The independent Commonwealth countries of Africa (including Mauritius), the Caribbean and the Pacific are offered the choice of three types of connection : association under the Yaoundé 'model' comparable to that of Francophone Africa and Somalia, including the offer of EDF aid; association under the Arusha 'model' comparable to that of the three East African Community countries; or a special trading agreement on specific commodities of interest.

A fairly large and heterogeneous group of countries are now either associated with, or have special trade agreements with, the Community[1]. The aims of association with the Community are different

[1]These fall into the following categories :
  i) Greece, Turkey, Malta – association agreements aimed at eventual full membership of the EEC. Cyprus in process of negotiation.
  ii) Morocco, Tunisia – association agreements not aimed at membership. Algeria in process of negotiation.
  iii) Yaoundé – association of 18 African and Malagasy states.
  iv) Arusha – association of 3 East African Community states.
  v) Spain – 6-year preferential trade agreement.
  vi) Yugoslavia – non-preferential trade agreement mainly aimed at exports of 'baby beef' to EEC market.

Continued on page 94

for 'European' countries (broadly defined) than for others; in respect of 'European' countries, it appears to be generally accepted that association is a process which should eventually lead to Community membership while, in respect of non-European countries, the policy followed has been one of 'transposing on to the Community level special links which certain African and Mediterranean countries had with one or other of the Six . . . extending these links to countries in a similar situation'[1]. Thus, the principle on which association is offered to independent Commonwealth LDCs, established at the time of the signing of the first Yaoundé convention in 1963, is that countries with a 'comparable economic and production structure' to the existing 18 Yaoundé associates should be eligible for association. In practice, this 'comparability' criterion appears to be defined in terms of geographic size, stage of development (widely construed to include countries as diverse as Zambia and the Gambia) and, implicitly, geographical location. All the Asian countries, which include the largest and some of the poorest Commonwealth developing countries, are regarded by the Community as non-associables. (See Table 6.1, where the population, per caput GNP and British official aid receipts of the 'associables' and 'non-associables' are detailed.)

The three main features of the Yaoundé association agreement are reciprocal trade preferences; a structure of mutual institutions, established on a basis of parity between the Six and the associates (the Eighteen), for administering the association; and aid provided through the EDF. The Arusha agreement makes no provision for EDF aid.

Reciprocal Trade Preferences
In Community practice a clear distinction is drawn between a simple trading agreement and a formal treaty of association. 'On the trade side, association is based on the principle of the establishment of a free trade area with reciprocal rights and obligations, to the extent that the latter can be assumed by developing countries'[2]. Thus, where Community preferences are granted to imports from associates, associates are also required to grant a measure of reverse preference to imports from the Community. Reverse preferences have been one of the most controversial elements of EEC agreements with LDCs, particularly in the context of relations with the US, which has opposed

[1]C. A. Cosgrove, 'The EEC and the Developing World', *European Community*. February 1971, p.14.
[2]Gerhard Schiffler, in *Britain, the EEC and the Third World*, ODI, July 1971, p.48.

vii) Israel – trade agreement.
viii) Egypt, Lebanon – negotiating trade agreements.
ix) Argentina – trade agreement. Uruguay in process of negotiation.
x) In addition, other non-member European countries (e.g. Austria, Portugal, Switzerland) may gain preferential access to the enlarged Community.

the practice throughout; to the extent that the US has refused to extend any General Preference scheme which it may bring in, to any LDC which continues to grant reverse preferences after 1975.

The Community's insistence on the free trade area principle is claimed to derive from the provisions of GATT[1] which prohibit the establishment of new preferential arrangements while allowing the establishment of free trade areas and customs unions covering a substantial proportion of trade between the parties. However, since 1964 GATT has waived this provision in the case of trade between developed and developing countries[2] (thus clearing the way for the establishment of General Preferences). Nevertheless, in negotiations leading up to the Arusha agreement and the abortive agreement with Nigeria, the concept of reverse preferences played a major role. Certainly in the East African case the concession of reciprocity, a major departure from previous East African trading practice, was a necessary pre-condition for association negotiations even to be started.

But despite the Community's insistence on the principle of reciprocity in negotiations with new associates, so far the actual value of reciprocal preferences granted may in many cases be rather small.

> 'In principle, the Eighteen grant similar concessions to imports from the Community but Yaoundé II, like its predecessors, allows the Eighteen to retain or introduce customs duties and charges with equivalent effect to meet development or budgetary needs, as long as such measures do not discriminate between the Community countries. The Eighteen are also allowed to retain or introduce quantitative restrictions on imports of Community products, in order to meet development needs or to alleviate balance of payments difficulties[3].'

Similar provisions enforced in the Arusha agreement have resulted in the creation of low 'most favoured nation' (mfn) customs tariffs, on which duty preferences are granted to EEC suppliers, and high 'fiscal duties' which apply to imports from all sources[4].

To argue that reciprocity is a necessary part of an association agreement, when in many cases it appears that the reciprocity granted in practice is merely 'formal', appears a rather odd doctrine. On the one hand, if reverse preferences have any practical value, they appear now to be contrary to the resolutions adopted in 1964 by UNCTAD and

Article XXIV.

See I. W. Zartman, *The Politics of Trade Negotiations between Africa and the European Economic Community*, pp.97-98.

Cosgrove, op. cit., p.16.

e.g.:—Vermouths etc., bottled: fiscal levy Shs. 19/- (East African shillings) per gallon or 66⅔%; full 'customs' duty Shs. 1/-; EEC rate free. Radios, TVs, radiograms: fiscal levy Shs. 50/- each or 47%; full 'customs' duty 3%; EEC rate free.

Table 6.1 British Dependencies and Independent Commonwealth Developing Countries

'Associable' Dependencies

Country	Population thousands	P/C GNP £	UK ODA[1] £'000
Bahamas	169	608	8
Bermuda	51	1,112	3
Brit. Antarctic	..	..	..
B. Honduras	122	162	2,263
B. Indian Ocean	1	..	..
B. Solomon Is.	160	80	3,318
B. Virgin Is.	9	..	636
Brunei	130	380	5
Cayman Is.	10	..	240
Cen. & Southern Line Is.	..	..	..
Falklands	3	..	7
Gilbert & Ellice	55	170	46
Montserrat	12	..	840
New Hebrides	81	..	615
Pitcairn Is.	..	..	1,199
St. Helena	5	..	428
Seychelles	52	30	1,656
Turks & Caicos	7	..	545
W. Indies Assoc.	500	..	6,375
Total or Average[3]	1,367	..	18,184

'Associable' Independents

Country	Population thousands	P/C GNP £	UK ODA[1] £'000
Barbados	250	190	598
Botswana	650	40	2,686
Cyprus	650	290	149
Fiji	530	140	2,346
Gambia	360	40	358
Ghana	8,800	100	5,182
Guyana	760	130	3,063
Jamaica	2,000	210	831
Lesotho	900	35	636
Malawi	4,500	25	7,181
Mauritius	810	90	1,553
Nigeria	66,000	40	8,698
Sierra Leone	2,600	60	619
Swaziland	420	70	2,316
Trinidad	1,100	300	497
Tonga	85	120	484
W. Samoa	150	55	8
Zambia	4,300	130	2,425
Malta[2]	330	240	7,204
Kenya[2]	10,800	55	9,804
Uganda[2]	9,800	45	3,623
Tanzania[2]	13,300	35	1,231
Total or Average[3]	129,100	55	61,492

'Non-Associables'

Country	Population thousands	P/C GNP £	UK ODA[1] £'000
Ceylon	12,500	60	4,298
Gibraltar	29	270	1,106
India	550,400	30	36,130
Malaysia	10,900	140	4,806
Nauru	6	..	..
Pakistan[4]	130,200	45	8,918
Singapore	2,100	290	7,689
Hong Kong	4,100	300	162
Total or Average[3]	739,200	35	62,785

Notes:
1. 1970, net of amortisation.
2. Already associated with EEC.
3. Weighted by population.
4. Figures for Bangladesh not separately available.

.. Not available.

Source: World Bank Publications.
British Aid Statistics, 1966–1970, HMSO, 1971
The United Kingdom and the European Communities, Cmnd. 4715, HMSO, 1971.

92

GATT; on the other hand, if they are merely 'formal' and in actual effect meaningless, why bother with them?

In practice it appears that the reciprocity principle has been used mainly in defence of the element of reciprocity in the Yaoundé convention, where existing preferences granted by the franc zone countries to France were extended to other Community members in return for their extension of preferences to these LDCs. In new association negotiations care has been taken to ensure that the benefits granted to the new associates do not outweigh those held by the Yaoundé countries, whose anxieties about the weakening of their own preferential ties with the Community through the enlargement of association (particularly since Yaoundé exports to the EEC have fallen relatively to those of other African countries) have limited the scope and speed of EEC action on LDC trade liberalisation. Hence, in the Nigerian and East African agreements, provisions are made for tariff quotas on goods which actively compete with those produced in Yaoundé countries (coffee, cloves and canned pineapples in the East African case), while the Yaoundé influence may also have affected the scope for concessions on agricultural goods in the Community's General Preference scheme[1].

Joint Institutions

The institutional provisions are regarded both by the Community and by associates as constituting the second most important element of an association agreement. The major institution established under both Yaoundé and Arusha is an Association Council composed of members from both 'groups'. Yaoundé lays down parity of voting in the Council between the Community and the Eighteen. Arusha is less specific: 'The Association Council shall act by mutual agreement between the European Economic Community on the one hand and the Partner States of the East African Community on the other[2].' However, in addition to the Council, Yaoundé also established an Association Committee, a Parliamentary Conference and a Court of Arbitration: a much more elaborate formal structure than is provided by Arusha.

Historically, this administrative structure derives from the 'General Secretariat for the Community and for African and Malagasy affairs' which linked the French Community with Paris. It is often claimed that the maintenance of the administrative framework makes it easier for mutual interests to be identified and points of disagreement to be solved. But, from outside, it is hard to see how far the presence of institutions as such has conferred benefits on associates beyond what might be expected from normal bilateral negotiation. The situation can perhaps be compared to that of the less formalised Commonwealth Secretariat structure which provides a useful forum for discussion of

[1] See below p.109.
[2] Arusha Agreement, 1969, Title IV, Article 24.

93

mutual interests and conflicts but which could be overridden by a British government determined to tread a separate path.

The European Development Fund (EDF)

Aid from the Community as a group is the third main element in association policy. The EDF has been the main channel of such aid to the Yaoundé associates, although no such funds are committed to the East African associates. In principle, Britain has agreed to contribute to EDF financing from 1975 (the start of the Fourth Fund)[1]. The size of the contribution, and its effect on the British aid programme, will depend in practice on the number of Commonwealth 'associables' which elect to join in a Yaoundé-type association.

EDF aid still forms only a small proportion of the total aid disbursements of Community countries. In 1969, the total value of the EEC's bilateral and Community overseas development assistance (net of amortisation) to the Yaoundé associates and dependencies was $797m (nearly 40% of total disbursements); of this, $120m (6% of the total) was disbursed through Community institutions[2]. Table 6.2 shows how the aid from the Community was directed in the period 1968-70. It is clear from this that bilateral flows, apart from those of France and Belgium, were mainly directed to countries outside Yaoundé. 57% of net flows from Germany, Italy and the Netherlands, moreover, were disbursed outside Africa. Contributions by member states to multilateral institutions are as large as, or larger than, their contributions to Community institutions

By comparison, in 1970 the 'associables' received 48% of total British bilateral overseas development assistance (net of amortisation). One estimate of the future British contribution to EDF[3] puts it at between £22m and £37m per annum, the upper and lower limits being governed by whether only British dependencies are covered by the enlarged Fund, or whether it extends to all 'associables'. (It is assumed that the UK contribution to EDF IV financing will be equal to those of France and West Germany, at 22% of the enlarged Fund.) This represents between 11% and 19% of gross, and between 15% and 26% of 'true net'[4] aid programme disbursements during 1970.

It is not yet clear whether a contribution by Britain to the EDF – of whatever size – would be made by an addition to the British aid programme or by a switch of funds from bilateral aid. The undertaking given by the original Six on the establishment of the first EDF

[1] The 1st EDF, established under the Rome Treaty, ran from 1958 to 1964; the 2nd ran from 1964 to 1970; the 3rd runs from 1971 to 1975.
[2] EDF and the European Investment Bank (EIB).
[3] Haruko Fukuda, 'Britain's Part in the European Development Fund', *National Westminster Bank Quarterly Review*, August 1971.
[4] i.e. net of amortisation and interest.

Table 6.2 EEC Bilateral and Community Official Development Assistance, 1968-1970 Annual Average, Net of Amortisation

$m

Destination	Belgium	France	Germany	Holland	Italy	Total Bilateral	Community[1]	Total
1. French Dependencies	—	282·2	—	—	—	282·2	6·8	289·0
2. Other Franc Area in Africa								
N. of Sahara	4·0	130·5	28·9	0·7	6·4	170·5	3·3	173·8
S. of Sahara	1·1	258·1	21·8	0·7	2·7	284·4	98·4	382·8
3. Other Africa	67·3	—	66·7	7·2	44·5	185·7	16·0	201·7
4. Americas	6·9	75·7[2]	61·2	40·4	-6·3	177·9	7·1	185·0
5. Asia	6·8	33·8[2]	216·2	55·0	42·9	354·7	10·4	365·1
6. Oceania	—	17·0[2]	—	—	—	17·0	2·2	19·2
7. Europe	1·1	32·9	89·5	3·5	17·0	144·0	34·7	178·7
8. Unallocated	1·1	28·1	26·6	23·7	2·2	81·7	—	81·7
(Total 3–8)	83·2	187·5	460·2	129·8	100·3	961·0	70·4	1,031·4)
9. Contributions to: EDF	12·3	43·9	43·9	11·8	17·8	129·7	—	129·7
Other Multilateral Orgs.	15·1	59·0	88·9	72·7	24·0	259·7	—	259·7
Total	115·7	961·2	643·7	215·7	151·2	2,087·5	178·9	2,266·4

Notes: 1. EDF + EIB.
2. Approximately adjusted to exclude French dependencies.

Source: DAC Review 1971, Tables Annex 6, 16, 17 and 18.

95

not to reduce the level of bilateral aid to prospective beneficiaries may create a precedent. If this were followed, then an EDF contribution as an addition to the aid budget would improve the relative position of associates at the expense of non-associates : a contribution which was deducted from other bilateral aid would put non-associated countries in an absolutely worse position. On the other hand, if this precedent were not followed and a British contribution to EDF were deducted from British bilateral aid to 'associables', no net difference in the position of non-associates would result.

The Community's view of EDF aid is that compared to bilateral assistance it has considerable advantages for LDCs; and this is no doubt the case for those countries eligible for it. The terms of reference are wide[1]; the terms are soft (90% of aid under the 3rd EDF is in the form of outright grants) and the EDF is prepared to enter joint ventures with other organisations, bilateral or multilateral, public or private, and to support local costs. Furthermore, the fact that procurement from EDF aid extends to purchases not only in the Community countries but also in any of the associates is a remarkably liberal feature. In practice, however, the principal beneficiary of procurement contracts under the EDF has continued, for mainly historical reasons, to be France. Table 6.3 shows the position at the end of 1969.

Table 6.3   **EEC Member States' Contributions to EDF and Contracts Gained from EDF, by End of 1969**

	Contributions		Contracts Gained			
	EDF I	EDF II	EDF I		EDF II	
	%	%	$'000	%	$'000	%
Belgium	12·05	9·45	10,683	2·6	22,259	8·8
W. Germany	34·4	33·75	19,686	4·9	58,049	22·9
France	34·4	33·75	185,767	45·7	98,781	39·0
Italy	6·9	13·7	52,590	12·9	25,218	10·0
Luxembourg	0·2	0·3	835	0·2	31	—
Netherlands	12·05	9·05	17,536	4·3	6,080	2·4
Associates[1]			118,791	29·2	43,109	17·0
Non-members			383	1·0	463	1·1
Total	100	100	406,266	100	253,080	100

Note: 1. Including EEC-owned firms registered in associates.
Source: *The European Development Fund: Access to Contracts,* European Communities Commission, 1970.

The EDF is sometimes criticised for the slowness of its procedures in actually disbursing funds. There are, as Table 6.4 shows, con-

[1] The EDF provisions of the first Yaoundé convention could cover infrastructure projects, agricultural price-stabilisation (to compensate for the abolition of the French colonial 'surprix' system), technical assistance, and aid to production and diversification. Under Yaoundé II, price stabilisation grants are abolished, although a reserve fund is established (up to $80m) against emergencies, such as a drastic fall in world prices or natural disasters. Aid to industrialisation is stressed, as are measures to encourage the marketing and sales promotion of products exported by the Eighteen.

siderable lags both between the time when money is made available to the EDF by member governments and the time when it is committed as aid, and also between commitment and disbursement. At the end of 1969, the Community had still not managed to spend the whole of the Fund set up under the Rome Treaty. And by mid-1970 it had disbursed only 44% of the 1964-69 Fund. If a larger proportion of British aid disbursements to the associable Commonwealth is to be directed through the EDF, careful transition period arrangements will have to be made in order to avoid a hiatus in aid disbursement to the recipients concerned.

Table 6.4   EDF and EIB Aid to Yaoundé Associates

	$m Funds Available	Commit- ments	Disburse- ments
1st EDF (1958–64)—Grants[1]	581·2	483·0	439·3
2nd EDF (1964–69)—Grants[1]	620·0	597·8	289·0
EDF Loans[1]	46·0	44·5	6·1
Total[1]	666·0	642·3	295·1
EIB Loans[2]	64·0	46·8	23·1
3rd EDF (1970–74)—Grants[1]	748·0	..	..
EDF Loans[1]	80·0	..	..
Total[1]	828·0	..	..
EIB Loans[2]	90·0	..	..

Notes: 1. Position at 30 June 1970.
2. Position at 31 December 1969.   .. Not available.
Source: Hansard, 26 April 1971.

The Non-Associables
It has been suggested, borrowing from an Indian context, that the correct term to use for 'non-associable' countries is 'Untouchables'; and the lack of any apparent development strategy towards Asia in the Community's thinking appears to put the continent firmly in this camp. Up till now, relations with developing countries outside the ambit of association agreements have been given very little considera- tion in official Community thinking. Formally, under the terms of the Treaty of Rome, only associates can be the subject of Community (as opposed to bilateral) aid policy, and relations with non-associated LDCs are dealt with by the Community's External Affairs Directorate, which covers *all* non-associate countries, including the developed ones.

This may have been adequate while the number and economic importance of associated states was limited to Yaoundé and to French and Dutch dependencies. But can such a structure suffice for an en- larged group of members and of related countries, covering a con- siderably larger proportion of world trade and aid flows? The Community's view of the situation is set out in a recent memorandum :

'The policy of preferential access which the Community pursues in its relations with some developing countries corresponds to special obligations and interests . . . .

97

'Co-operation of this type, however, is feasible only if it covers a relatively small proportion of world trade and if it is confined to countries in relatively homogeneous geographical areas.

'Taken beyond this point, the policy of association would tend to become diluted and would cease to be complementary to international co-operation; indeed it would be inimical to it because of the scale of the distortions and difficulties which it would lead to in world trade[1].'

An essential part of the concept of association, therefore, is that it should be restricted to a relatively small group of countries.

Commonwealth Asian countries, as non-associables, face the loss of preferential treatment in the British market and additional discrimination through the new duty-free treatment granted by the larger number of EEC member countries to each other, as well as to a widening ring of regional associates. The Community's view is that this additional loss is compensated for by the extension of generalised preferences; but only if, as a second Community memorandum[2] points out, all other industrial countries extend generalised preferences on a similar scale to that offered by the EEC. The exclusion of textile and leather products from most of the schemes proposed, and the lack of action in the United States, places the large Commonwealth Asian states in a poor position, first as a result of the quotas for 'sensitive' products in the EEC generalised preference system[3] (while associates' exports gain unrestricted access) and secondly in view of the possible effects of Common Agricultural Policy variable levies on agricultural exports[4].

Both India and Pakistan have had special trading agreements with the EEC covering specific products of interest (jute, coir, handicrafts and cotton textiles). Both countries have also been hoping to extend these into general trade agreements ensuring access to the market of the enlarged Community, and have opened negotiations on this basis; but progress so far has been slow, particularly in the sensitive sectors of jute and coir products where it has been the Community's view that the interests of the (declining) domestic industry must be preserved. Whether a general trading agreement will, in the end, emerge, and what the terms will be, is as yet not clear. However,

[1]See *Commission Memorandum on a Community Development Co-operation Policy: Summary Document*, Supplement 5/71 – Annex to the Bulletin of the European Communities 9/10 – 1971, pp. 26-27.
[2]*Communication de la Commission au Conseil concernant les relations entre I. La Communauté et l'Inde: II. La Communauté et l'Iran: III. La Communauté et le Pakistan*, European Communities Commission Memorandum No. SEC (71)2922 final, 28 July 1971.
[3]See below, p.109.
[4]See below, p.104 ff.

the treatment which countries like India, Pakistan and Bangladesh may receive from an enlarged EEC is foreshadowed in the Memorandum on development policy[1]. Here a system of 'co-operation agreements', forming a kind of half-way stage between full association and the general treatment of LDCs, is suggested; but it is not clear exactly how this would operate, and no specific proposals are made.

The Common Agricultural Policy (CAP)

The products in which the developing countries' share in world trade is falling most rapidly are primary and processed agricultural commodities[2]. This is particularly the case for products, such as wheat, sugar, oils and fats, where developed and developing countries compete. To a large extent, all developed countries have shielded their agricultural sector (frequently the most vulnerable part of the economy) from foreign competition, by a variety of measures and for a variety of reasons. One of the most common and, apparently, most successful arguments used by the farming lobby in developed countries has been that of the 'strategic' need to maintain or increase self-sufficiency in food products (a particularly attractive argument in Britain's case) : other reasons for protection of agriculture may be social (the wish to arrest a drain of people from country to town) or overtly political (the need for a government to rely on the rural vote).

Any kind of protection of production of any commodity, in any country or group of countries, represents a distortion of the alleged ideal of global free trade; and all developed countries protect their farmers. Similarly, any arrangement which favours one foreign source of supply over another (for whatever reason) distorts international trade. But what has been recognised – from the start by the critics of the CAP and at last, within the Community, in the Mansholt Plan – is the extremely high cost both to the consumer and to governments of operating the Community's agricultural policy, *plus* the great distortions which its pricing mechanism creates in world trade. Furthermore, the entry of the United Kingdom (a net importer of most foods) into the Community (a net exporter) seems likely to provide a further spur to internal European production at the expense of EEC consumers and taxpayers, as well as foreign exporters. Until recently, British policy sought a three-way balance between public support for agriculture through the tax system, the encouragement of domestic production, and regular supplies of imported food. This led to low tariffs on most agricultural goods (with preference given, in many cases, to Commonwealth suppliers) and these arrangements were

[1] *A Community Development Co-operation Policy*, EEC, 1971, p.29.
[2] See Chapter 1.

frequently supplemented by specific agreements with other traditional suppliers such as Denmark and Ireland.

But, as John Southgate points out in his Fabian pamphlet, Government policy since 1970:

> 'seems to have a triple intention: to encourage domestic production, to move the cost of agricultural support from direct to indirect taxation and to bring Britain closer to the Six. It is not easy to foresee in any detail the effects of this change on international trade . . . but it is relevant to point out that if domestic prices are high, variable levies are a most effective way, short of a total ban, of limiting freedom to import. . . . Only when the home producer has supplied all he can, will there be room for imports: the would-be supplier can therefore never plan his production and exports with any certainty. Moreover, variable levies destroy any relation between prices for imports and for domestic produce; the outside supplier is therefore unable to influence price or the level of consumption on the importing market[1]'.

The main commodity groups in which different LDCs are harmed by the CAP's operations are grains (including rice – see Chapter 1); beef products (on which the Community has negotiated a special trading agreement with Argentina); fruit and vegetables, including canned fruit (potentially important for many LDCs, including some in Africa and Asia); oilseeds, including cakes and meals made from oilseeds; and sugar – the commodity to which perhaps most attention has been paid during the pre-entry negotiations.

The basic system of protection is broadly the same for all CAP products[2]. Protection for Community producers is provided by the operation of the variable levies which make up the difference between world market prices and 'reference', 'sluicegate' or 'threshold' prices (a notional minimum duty-paid import price, calculated by the Community Commission from the 'target', 'basic' or 'guide' prices which form the basis of the farm price support system within the Community). Associates may in some cases receive preferences on CAP levies as well as on customs duties. However, although customs preferences for associates can only be varied after prior consultation with the associates, the depth of preference granted on CAP levies is variable at the discretion of the EEC authorities without such consultation.

[1] John Southgate, *Agricultural Trade and the EEC*, Fabian Research Series No. 294, May 1971.
[2] For descriptions of the system see Michael Butterwick and Edmund Neville Rolfe, *Food, Farming and the Common Market*, OUP, 1968; *Britain, the EEC and the Third World*, ODI, 1971.

It has been claimed that 'In Britain's third attempt to enter the EEC, perhaps no other factor has worked more in her favour than the vast market she offers Europe for the disposal of farm surpluses[1].' Certainly, as Table 6.5 shows, trends in EEC food imports since the establishment of the CAP in 1965 seem to bear out clearly a tendency towards self-sufficiency.

The greatest relative falls in this period were in imports of these goods from the US, EFTA and Canada. This has encouraged the view that since those most strongly affected are high-income producers, who protect their own farming sectors, disruption of trade in CAP commodities – mainly temperate – does not matter overmuch to developing countries. But to say this is to ignore the degree of competition which can exist between differing but competitive goods produced in temperate and tropical regions[2]. The most crucial examples are vegetable oilseeds, oils, sugar and rice[3].

It is well known that many temperate and tropical vegetable oils derived from different types of crop are close substitutes[4]. Customs duties in the Community rise by stage of production, with oilseeds and oilseed cake entering duty-free but import duties of up to 20% levied on vegetable oils. In addition, under the CAP, a subsidy amounting to the difference between a Community 'target price' and the lowest ruling cif import price, determined weekly, is paid to oilseed crushers, while a basic 'intervention price' some way below the target is guaranteed to domestic producers. As long as domestic supplies of oilseeds can be bought for less than the target price, the subsidy ensures that local produce is cheaper than that from abroad. The high level at which intervention prices were fixed has considerably encouraged Community production of oilseeds, which rose by some 55% between 1966/67 and 1969/70, and the proportion of EEC consumption supplied locally has continued to rise in a rapidly growing market. But a strong increase in imports from the United States and Eastern Europe has contributed largely to the exclusion of LDCs from the market. It is thought that the entry of the UK to the system will provide a further stimulus to production both in Britain and in the Community.

Among Commonwealth LDCs, the main suppliers of oilseeds and vegetable oils to the British market are among the 'associable' group of countries: Nigeria, the Gambia and Malawi, for example. India and Malaysia, however, also enjoy strong competitive positions. If

[1]A. L. Lougheed, 'The Common Agricultural Policy and International Trade', *National Westminster Bank Quarterly Review,* November 1971.
[2]FAO estimates that approximately half the agricultural exports of LDCs compete with protected production in developed countries. (*Indicative World Plan, 1970-1985.*)
[3]The case of rice is discussed in Chapter 1.
[4]See, e.g., Southgate, op.cit., pp.17-18; and M. P. Cracknell, *Journal of World Trade Law,* Vol. 2, No. 4, 1968.

Table 6.5 EEC Imports of Foodstuffs, Oils and Fats, 1965 and 1969¹

SITC Group	Group/Commodity	Total Imports by EEC Members 1965 $m	1969 $m	Imports from non-EEC Area 1965 $m	1969 $m	Share of Imports from EEC Members in Total 1965 %	1969 %
0—(07–073)	Competing Foodstuffs²	7,078	9,224	4,730	4,859	32·2	47·4
00	Live Animals	448	707	335	383	25·2	45·8
01	Meat Preparations	1,003	1,430	602	627	40·0	56·1
02	Dairy Products	531	772	200	110	62·3	85·8
03	Fish	382	475	300	342	21·4	28·0
04	Cereals	1,617	1,808	1,230	979	24·0	45·8
05	Fruit and Vegetables	2,137	2,619	1,360	1,546	36·4	41·1
06	Sugar, etc.	206	252	145	112	29·6	55·5
073	Chocolate, etc.	55	116	9	11	83·7	90·5
08	Fodder	643	947	533	728	17·1	23·1
09	Other Foodstuffs	55	103	15	24	72·7	76·5
4	Animal, Vegetable Oils and Fats	522	623	437	445	16·3	28·6

Notes: 1. Because wine is the only SITC Group 1 commodity covered by the CAP, and it appears only since November 1969, Group 1 is excluded from the table.
2. 0—(07–073) = total foodstuffs (0) minus 'non-competing' tropical foodstuffs: coffee, cocoa, and tea (07–073).

Source: A. L. Lougheed, op. cit.
Commodity Trade Statistics, UN, various issues.

the present Community policies continue in operation, enlargement of the Community is likely to raise new barriers in the UK market against exports of vegetable oils from Asian countries as a result of the concession of preferential duty-free entry to new African associates[1]. But in addition, the provisions of the CAP, outlined above, may raise even more insuperable obstacles to exports of oilseeds from 'associables' and 'non-associables' alike.

The complete lack of attention which the plight of oilseed-producing LDCs received in the negotiations for entry provides a marked contrast to the vocal, and at least partially successful, campaign on cane sugar. Access for cane sugar to the UK market is guaranteed by restrictions on the acreage which can be used for beet farming. The price which will be paid for Commonwealth imports is also guaranteed under the Commonwealth Sugar Agreement (CSA). By contrast, EEC agricultural policy provides no such guarantee of market access or of price. There are, exceptionally, 'transitional' national beet sugar production quotas in the Community, but surpluses amounting to some 11% of EEC consumption have still arisen[2]. While the cane producers of French Overseas Departments (DOM) – principally, in this case, Réunion, Guadeloupe and Martinique – benefit from treatment equivalent to that given to European beet producers, this is not the case for other associates, who receive no CAP levy preferences.

The position of Commonwealth sugar is due to be reviewed in 1974, on the expiry of the present CSA. The Community has undertaken to 'take to heart' the interests of Commonwealth producers when new arrangements for an enlarged EEC are worked out after 1974, but plainly much will depend on the UK Government's attitude to these negotiations at the time. Although many conflicting estimates of the enlarged Community's surplus or deficit have been made, the outcome of the extension of the CAP to the Ten, failing the introduction of effective production quotas, is likely to be a marked increase in Community output. Southgate[3] argues that, when the UK market is opened to EEC exporters, the Community sugar surplus which is now largely converted into animal feed could easily be sold as refined sugar.

Either of two policies might be followed in order to safeguard the interests of cane sugar producers : to bring developing Commonwealth production under the wing of the CAP (like the DOM) or to institute a really effective production quota on Community beet production. Of the two, the former would be considerably more expensive for the EEC budget, since it would involve extending the system of target and

[1]Although the degree of preference may be limited by tariff quotas (e.g. as proposed in the abortive Nigerian agreement).
[2]This is because the Community's quotas limit the quantity of sugar which will gain a guaranteed market and price (in contrast to Britain's absolute limit on acreage available).
[3]Southgate, op. cit.

intervention prices and export subsidies. Moreover, by widening the scope of price support without production controls, it could provide an incentive for even greater excess production, and risk the complete flooding of the (already residual) world market.

The question remains : How can an enlarged Community reconcile the conflicting interests of its farmers, its consumers, and the rest of the world? It is fairly clear that the interests of non-farm consumers lie in a food supply system which provides goods at the lowest cost. In so far as this can be achieved by policies which respect the principle of comparative advantage and which can permit the expansion of profitable export-oriented agriculture in developing countries, the interests of EEC consumers and of LDCs coincide. Tax subsidies to domestic farmers through deficiency payments or through artifically high domestic prices with discrimination against imports may be equally effective in protecting European agriculture from imported competition; but the former, in conjunction with a progressive income tax, is more equitable than the latter, which bears hardest on the poor. In either event, the maintenance of domestic production quotas will probably be necessary if market access for LDC produce is to be assured.

Although it is clearly not in the interests of the majority of the UK population – nor in those of a high proportion of the population of the EEC – to maintain a high-cost, surplus-creating, import-excluding farm system, the pressures acting against effective EEC agricultural reform, the lack of agreement in the Six over the Mansholt Plan, and, in particular, the limitations imposed on the Mansholt proposals to reduce the acreage and working population in Community agriculture, emphasise the difficulties involved. It is unlikely that it will be easier to achieve reforms of this kind in a ten-member Community; yet without such reforms the outlook for developing countries will remain bleak.

General Preferences in an Enlarged Community

The harmonisation of customs tariffs among the proposed ten-member Community will imply the unification of the members' offers of generalised preferences. At present, the UK, the Community and Norway each operate separate and differing schemes, and it is expected that the UK system will be altered to that of the Community by 1974.

In principle, Britain has agreed to adopt the structure of the scheme put into action by the EEC in July 1971. It is fairly clear that, leaving textile policy aside, the move will be to a system which appears, in principle, markedly less generous than the present UK offer, which itself has many notable exclusions[1].

[1]See Appendix B. For a detailed outline of the UK system, see *Trade and Industry*, HMSO, 23 September 1971, p.578, and 14 October 1971, p.62. For the Community system, see UNCTAD document TD/B.373/Add.1.

Comparison of the Schemes

Under the British scheme the countries and dependencies listed in Appendix C are regarded as eligible for general preferential (GSP) treatment, provided their goods adhere to statutory conditions on origin and consignment[1]. All manufactures and semi-manufactures in Brussels Tariff Nomenclature Chapters 25-99 are covered, excepting cotton textiles and goods on which excise duties are levied[2]. In the majority of cases, duties are completely eliminated, and no *ex ante* quota restrictions or ceilings are built into the system. For agricultural and processed agricultural goods, the scheme covers a limited range of items, estimated at approximately 14% of Britain's imports of these goods from non-Commonwealth LDCs. Again, for the majority, the existing import duty is entirely eliminated. Commonwealth preferences continue as before.

As a safeguard clause, the United Kingdom reserves the right to withdraw or modify the preferential tariff treatment if a product is imported 'in such increased quantities and under such conditions, as a result of the preference, as to cause or threaten in the opinion of the United Kingdom Government serious injury to domestic producers of like or directly competitive products'[3].

The structure of the Community's scheme is at once much more complex and much more precise than that introduced by Britain. It is divided into five parts :—

List I	BTN 25-99 manufactures and semi-manufactures, except those separately listed.
List II	Items covered by the GATT Long Term Arrangement on cotton textiles.
List III	Other textiles, plus footwear.
List IV	Agricultural goods (BTN 1-24).
List V	Iron and steel products in the European Coal and Steel Community regime.

The concepts of tariff quotas *(plafonds)* and country ceilings *(butoirs)* are central to the system as it applies to manufactures and semi-manufactures. In principle, the tariff quotas and ceilings apply to all manufactures covered by the scheme. In practice, however, a distinction is made between sensitive, quasi-sensitive and non-sensitive goods, depending on the degree to which goods are held to be competitive with EEC domestic manufactures, tariff quotas being held in reserve *(quotas fictifs)* for non-sensitive and quasi-sensitive items. In

[1]See *Trade and Industry*, 14 October 1971, p.62. The rules of origin are designed to coincide very closely with those operating in the EEC.
[2]Any item containing hydrocarbon oils; perfumed spirits; matches; and portable cigarette lighters.
[3]*Trade and Industry*, 23 September 1971, p.578.

these cases, the Community Commission, on its own judgement of whether the level of imports is actively harming EEC interests, has the right to decide whether or not the tariff quotas should be enforced.

Each of the five lists carries different regulations regarding quotas and ceilings :—

> *Lists I and V* All listed LDCs[1] are covered by the scheme. Tariff quotas on sensitive commodities are calculated as equal to 1968 cif imports by value from beneficiaries, excluding associates, plus 5% of imports in the most recent year for which figures are available (in practice 1969 for 1971) from all other extra-Community sources, including associates. This tariff quota (the *plafond*) is the level of imports allowed in duty-free; and subsequent imports carry the full duty. The country ceilings which govern the duty-free allowance for any one exporting country (the *butoirs*) vary[2], and in addition, the tariff quotas are allocated proportionately among the importing member states[3]. If the allocation for any member state is exceeded, subsequent imports in the same year carry the full duty. These country quotas are not transferable.
>
> *List II* Only the less developed members of the GATT Long Term Arrangement on Cotton Textiles (Colombia, India, Jamaica, South Korea, Mexico, Pakistan and Egypt) benefit. The tariff quotas enforced on sensitive items are limited to the tonnage of deliveries during 1968 from the beneficiaries alone, and country ceilings are fixed at 30% of the tariff quota except in the case of cotton undergarments (50%). Quotas are allocated amongst the member states in the same proportions as in List I.
>
> *List III* Only independent countries can benefit from GSP preferences on this list (thus Hong Kong is excluded). Quota levels on sensitive items are determined as in List I; the country ceiling is 30% in most cases, except for leather footwear, undergarments and carpets with under 350 rows of knots per square metre (20%) and carpets with over 500 rows of knots per square metre (50%). Textile quotas are calculated by weight and footwear by value.
>
> *List IV*, concerning agricultural goods in BTN 1-24, is differently administered : only a selection of goods have been included and only partial duty reductions given, the unweighted average cut in tariff being about one-third. CAP levies are unaffected. There

[1]See Appendix C.
[2]The *butoir* for 12 items is 50% of the *plafond;* for 7, 30%; for 24, 20%; and for 1 (basketwork, wickerwork etc.) 10%.
[3]In the following ratio : Germany 37.5%, France 27.1%, Italy 20.3%, Benelux 15.1%.

are no quotas but there is an escape clause which allows the reintroduction of the full tariff in the interests of either associate or domestic producers.

It is claimed by the EEC Commission that the tariff quotas provided, in 1971, duty-free access for more than twice the value of the Community's dutiable imports from eligible LDCs in 1968, the base year. While, statistically, this is so, the situation of 'sensitive' and 'quasi-sensitive' commodities, where *plafonds* and *butoirs* really count, is considerably less liberal. Here, the duty-free quotas for 1971 amounted to $345m as against imports of $270m in 1968, an increase of some 28%.

In 1970, the value of *total* exports from LDCs into the Community was already 26% higher than in 1968. Richard Cooper[1] has argued that, projecting past growth-rates, imports of broad groups of products (chemicals, semi-finished manufactures and 'miscellaneous' manufactures) may soon exceed the *plafonds*, even if they are not modified by the *butoirs*. Thus, he argues, 'if actual exports exceed the quota ceiling, so that mfn duties must be paid on the excess, then there will be no new incentive where it counts, at the margin'[2], to stimulate investment for export manufacture in developing countries.

Nevertheless, the creation of new tariff-free quotas where none existed before can, it is admitted, be an incentive to increase exports. And the fact that the EEC's system is the only one to include cotton textiles, however restrictively, is a point in its favour. But the value quota system enforced in most cases may well encourage LDCs to cut prices to the bone in competition for shares of the quota. 'Producers in developing countries may compete with one another sufficiently to bid down the sales price even on duty-free imports to the point prevailing on dutiable products. Under these . . . circumstances, the real beneficiaries of the . . . scheme will be the European importers lucky enough to get the duty-free quotas[3].' Similar distortions may result, in the context of global quotas, from the provision that each member 'shall guarantee for importers of the products concerned established in its territory free access to the share allotted to it'[4]. On the one hand, in conditions of competitive supply (particularly where there are monopolistic buyers) such a measure coupled with a quota system, although liberal in expression, may again put a premium on price-cutting; on the other hand, where non-competitive trade flows exist (e.g. between an overseas subsidiary and a European parent company) it does nothing to minimise the importance of such connections.

[1]R. N. Cooper, *The European Communities' System of Generalised Tariff Preferences: A Critique*, Yale University Economic Growth Centre Discussion Paper No. 132, November 1971.
[2]Ibid., p.10.
[3]Ibid., p.8.
[4]EEC Council Regulation No. 1308/71, June 1971, Article 3.2.

Within a system of global quotas, exporting country ceilings (the *butoirs*) are necessary in order to protect the interests of less competitive LDCs. It is fairly clear that, without this provision, the principal beneficiaries of the EEC system in 1971 (Yugoslavia, Iran, India, Pakistan and Brazil in particular) would have exhausted practically all the *plafonds*. Moreover, in establishing the system in this way, the Community has followed the proposal made originally in UNCTAD with the aim of giving special preferences to the 'least developed' countries. Nevertheless, it is perhaps only because of the existence of global quotas that the need for exporters' ceilings assumes such importance; and it is possible that this measure and the allocation of import quotas among the member states may only create further uncertainties for LDCs. As far as the latter measure is concerned, if several LDCs are competing under the scheme in exporting to several of the EEC countries, none of them is likely to know at what points the import quotas of any one country are likely to be exhausted. Since there is no provision for the spreading of quotas over the year, there will be pressure on the LDCs to crowd their exports as near as possible to the beginning of the year, in order to get into the market before the allocations are filled. Although, by virtue of free internal transfer within the EEC, goods which have reached the import quota in one country may still enter duty-free if they can be brought through another area whose quota has not been filled, such a procedure adds extra freight, wharfage and time costs to trade.

Apart from these restrictive factors, the scheme seems administratively very complex and expensive. Perhaps the most complicated element is the inspection system for 'quasi-sensitive' goods for which, when the *plafond* is reached, a decision must be made on whether or not to reimpose the tariff. This involves the rapid transmission of import data by Telex from ports of entry to a central monitoring bureau, and the need for equally rapid assessment of the data, before the system can be fully effective. The establishment of such a system creates another considerable call on the Community administrative budget.

The entry of Britain and the three other new members to the Community will alter the basis for the calculation of *plafonds* and *butoirs* by removing imports from the four into the Six (previously part of the supplementary quota) from the calculation, and counting them as 'intra-Community' trade. The exact calculation of 'basic' and 'supplementary' tariff quotas will also depend on the number and importance of new associates. Cooper[1] has estimated that an enlarged scheme might be slightly less restrictive than that of the 'Six' alone. Meanwhile, ODI is carrying out an analysis of the effects of an enlarged EEC scheme on the six 'non-associable' Commonwealth Asian LDCs. As a

[1]Cooper, op.cit.

Table 6.6   EEC Imports from Commonwealth Asia by Class of GSP Treatment, 1968

$'000

BTN Chapters/Classes		India	%	Pakistan	%	Ceylon	%	Malaysia	%	Singapore	%	Hong Kong	%	Total	%
1–24:	Duty-free	13,948	40	6,618	85	54	—	5,582	26	2,222	25	1,289	33	29,713	30
	Excluded from Offer	18,439	53	784	10	22,655	99	15,116	71	6,667	75	1,615	42	65,276	66
	Included in Offer[1]	2,393	7	388	5	279	1	481	2	36	—	982	25	4,559	4
	Total	34,780	100	7,790	100	22,988	100	21,179	100	8,925	100	3,886	100	99,548	100
25–99:	Duty-free	88,915	72	77,708	71	10,186	95	140,543	96	13,439	87	16,556	11	347,347	63
List II:	Sensitive	1,833	1	2,189	2	—	—	—	—	—	—	—	—	4,022	1
	Non-sensitive	560	—	91	—	—	—	—	—	—	—	—	—	651	—
Others:	Sensitive	3,719	3	2,350	2	13	—	683	1	405	3	32,410	22	39,580	7
	Non-sensitive	12,270	10	20,081	19	522	5	4,541	3	1,389	9	11,676	8	50,479	9
	Jute & Coir	16,343	13	5,743	5	11	—	—	—	—	—	17	—	22,114	4
	Excluded	—	—	—	—	—	—	37[2]	—	197[2]	1	87,266[3]	59	87,500	15
	Total	123,640	100	108,162	100	10,732	100	145,804	100	15,430	100	147,925	100	551,693	100
Grand Total		158,420		115,952		33,720		166,983		24,355		151,811		651,241	

Notes: 1. Counting parts of tariff items, for which statistics are not available, as whole items (i.e. overstating).
2. LTA cotton textiles (List II).
3. All textiles and footwear (Lists II and III).

Source: *Analytical Tables of Trade for the European Communities 1968* (NIMEXE), European Communities Statistical Office.

109

first stage, the values of imports subject to GSP treatment into the EEC from these countries in 1968 (the base year) have been calculated; and these are summarised in Table 6.6[1]. The wide variation in the situation of each individual country should be noted but, averaging out, the following emerges. For agricultural goods (BTN 1-24) 30% of imports were in duty-free classes and, of the rest, 93% were in classes excluded from GSP treatment. For BTN 25-99, 63% of imports were in duty-free classes. Of the rest, 53% were excluded from the offer on various disqualifications, and 21% were regarded as sensitive, leaving only 26% of dutiable EEC imports of manufactures from Commonwealth Asia subject to 'non-sensitive' treatment under the EEC preference scheme.

It is impossible to predict with any accuracy what the form of the eventual joint system will be, or how generous in terms of 'sensitive' treatment and of coverage of agricultural products it is likely to become. There is no doubt that the Community system, as it stands, contains restrictions and rigidities which are absent from the British scheme (as also from the proposals of the Scandinavian countries); but the measure of generosity in the enlarged '1974 model' system will depend entirely on the attitudes of EEC member countries (including Britain) during the review of the system to be undertaken in 1973[2]. Meanwhile, it will be necessary to watch carefully the operations of the two systems and the reactions of domestic industrial and agricultural pressure groups in Britain, as well as in the 'Six', to changes in import patterns which may result in 1972 from the operation of the GSP on either side.

Policies for the Future?

The negotiations which will take place between now and 1974, when the Yaoundé convention will be renewed, provide an opportunity for taking stock of the EEC's relations with the Third World in general. As is evident from the patchwork of policy proposals currently emerging from the Commission, there are many conflicting interests involved, on both sides. The proliferation of regional arrangements in the Mediterranean area is difficult to reconcile with the claims of German business interests in Latin America and, in turn, with the maintenance of special treatment for the Yaoundé group. The addition of the United Kingdom, with 'an impressive collection of visiting cards, all engraved

[1]Results are provisional.

[2]For example, a Community official has recently suggested that since the British scheme's offer on processed agricultural goods is 'distinctly more advantageous' than that of the EEC, it is therefore conceivable that it would be adopted by the Ten. (See Tran Van-thinh, 'A balance between Various Interests', *European Community*, January 1972, p.23.)

with the same family name, "The Commonwealth"[1], adds the final turn in the maze of special claims and special relationships.

It would be opportune if the accession of the UK, with its Commonwealth interests, to the Community, with its Yaoundé and regional interests, could provide a point at which such a general review of the enlarged EEC's policies towards developing countries could be undertaken. Broadly, the process embodies the reconciliation of two differing 'spheres of interest', based to a large extent on separate colonial histories. It is worth considering whether there is still relevance in the Community attitude to LDCs; i.e., that there exists a particular geographical and economic 'region' with which a European Community of ten members can identify itself. In particular, it should be asked whether the concept of association, which appears to be leading to three or four levels of preferential treatment for differing groups of countries, determined by criteria which are hard to justify in global terms, is one which is worth preserving.

To some extent, confusion in policy formulation towards LDCs arises from the present division of responsibilities between the Community authorities and national governments, where aid is largely a national policy question but trade policy emanates from the joint authority. Within a review of policies, then, the roles of bilateral, Community-multilateral and fully multilateral aid should be fully reviewed in the contexts of the meaning of association and of the extension of general trade concessions to LDCs by the Community authorities. At present, the issues and the responsibilities sometimes appear submerged in a flood of ad hoc measures brought in as a reaction to events, and the danger exists that global policy will merely be the sum of a large number of 'special cases'.

[1]Charles Schiffman, 'Global Tariff Preferences', *European Community*, February 1971.

7 Development - The Search for a New Strategy

by Guy Hunter

There has been a fall in the barometer of development expectations over the last two years. It was not so noticeable as it moved from 'Fair' to 'Change', but there are now more anxious glances as it moves to 'Rain', with 'Stormy' not so far away. Perhaps it stood highest when the Pearson Report was first published in 1969. At that moment we were, indeed, confronted with sterner demands to increase the international transfer of resources; but the aggregate GNP growth-rates *had* achieved an average of 5% per annum, and the additional task of raising aid targets to a full 1% of donor GNP, with 0.7% of GNP for official aid alone, was stiff but clearly not impracticable. except (in political terms) for the United States, the largest donor, and for one or two of the poorer donors.

A vigorous tap on the glass given by the Columbia University Conference (February 1970), which closely examined Pearson, showed the first sharp fall. It showed that the Pearson targets, even if achieved, would not prevent a faster widening of the gap between incomes in developed and developing countries; and it cast serious doubt on the value of GNP growth-rates as a measure of development. This attack on the GNP criterion was followed up by the ILO (Seers) Mission to Colombia, which took employment as a major index of desirable achievement, and at the ODA Conference on employment at Cambridge (September 1970). The points of chief concern became, not so much the rich-poor gap on a world basis, but the continuing poverty, malnutrition and under-employment of the poor. Studies by V. M. Dandekar[1] and B. S. Minhas[2] in India showed a positively 'stormy' prospect that, even on optimistic assumptions of success in the Indian Plan, over 40% of India's population – say 220m people – would be living below the poverty line of about 1 Rupee (5 new pence) per head per day at the end of the Plan period. By the time of the SID World Conference in Ottawa (May 1971), one of the most distinguished Pakistani planners, Mahbub ul Haq[3], was openly saying that perhaps the whole approach to planning, aimed at maximising aggregate GNP, was not in fact benefiting the poor, and that an entirely new principle of *direct* attack on poverty, malnutrition and

[1] V. M. Dandekar, *Poverty in India* (The Ford Foundation), New Delhi, December 1970.
[2] B. S. Minhas, *Mass Poverty and Strategy of Rural Development in India,* New Delhi, March 1971.
[3] Mahbub ul Haq, 'Employment in the 1970s; A New Perspective', SID World Conference, Ottawa, May 1971.

employment must be put in its place. He was not alone in this view.

Let us put together the gloomy factors which of late have been more brutally exposed. First, there are the population growth rates. The UN estimates for world population have been rising. The 1969 estimate for the year 2,000 gave :

More Developed Regions	1,441m
Less Developed Regions	4,671m
World	6,112m
[Present World	3,700m]

The 'recently calculated' estimate (UN Department of Social and Economic Affairs 'medium' projection 1970), again for the year 2,000, gave :

More Developed Regions	1,454m
Less Developed Regions	5,040m
World	6,494m

Whatever may be done about population control in the future, the 18-year-olds of 1990 are born already : it is only in projections beyond A.D. 2000 that LDCs could hope to alter present prospects substantially by action now. Mr. McNamara[1] has pointed out that, if LDCs could reach a net reproduction rate of one (an average of two children per couple) by A.D. 2040, their total population would still ultimately reach 13.9 billions; but that, if the net reproduction rate of one could be reached 20 years earlier, the ultimate LDC population would be only 9.6 billions – a difference of over 4 billions, i.e. more than the present population of the world.

Second, there are the employment figures. David Turnham[2] has estimated the growth of the labour force in less developed countries at 25.2% for the decade 1970-80 (2.3% p.a.), which means an absolute increase of roughly 250m in the decade; it is calculated that in India alone over 60m will be the net addition to the labour force in the same decade. Most of this labour force is young; and Elliot Berg[3] calculates that, excluding Latin America, only about 10% of it is in full-time wage-paid employment. Further, Turnham calculates that in 1950 73.3% of LDC population was in the agricultural sector, falling only to 70.7% in 1960 – i.e. a very slow rate of percentage structural change, and of course a large increase in *absolute* numbers

[1]Robert S. McNamara, *Address to the Board of Governors of the World Bank*, September 1971.
[2]David Turnham, *The Employment Problem in Less Developed Countries*, Paris, OECD Development Centre, June 1970.
[3]Elliot J. Berg, 'Wages and Employment', *The Challenge of Unemployment to Development*, Montebello (Canada) Conference; Paris, OECD Development Centre, 1971.

113

in the rural economy. Particularly for Africa and Asia, it is quite evident that no realistic estimate of the rate of growth of wage-paid employment, within the present development strategies, could possibly absorb even the already certain increases in the labour force, let alone reduce the present volume of unemployment. There are two possible implications – a steep rise in open, urban unemployment, and a steep rise in the number of people whom the rural economy will have to absorb; in fact, both town and country will suffer, in degrees varying from country to country.

Third, there is the question of poverty and of income distribution. As Mahbub ul Haq has said[1] :

> 'We are more aware now that the very pattern and organisation of production itself dictates a pattern of consumption and distribution which is politically very difficult to change. Once you have increased your GNP by producing more luxury houses and cars, it is not very easy to convert them into low cost housing or bus transport. A certain pattern of consumption and distribution inevitably follows.
>
> 'We have a number of case-studies by now which show how illusory it was to hope that the fruits of growth could be redistributed without reorganising the pattern of production and investment first. . . . In my own country, Pakistan, the very institutions we created for promoting faster growth and capital accumulation frustrated, later on, all our attempts for better distribution and greater social justice.'

In fact, the whole concept that GNP growth, concentrated in a small modern sector, would be diffused downwards through society fast enough to substantially improve living standards among the poor is now under grave suspicion, particularly in the countries where population growth is highest and where the proportion of rural to urban (or agricultural to industrial) distribution is highest.

The prospect of combined overcrowding, poverty and unemployment carries possibilities of violence and of disasters which cannot be wished away. In Pakistan itself, the revolt of the poorer East against the richer West resulted in civil war, and the poorer elements of the West are also in political revolt against the richer section.

At least, if storm signals are flying, there may be some encouragement in a growing reappraisal in development thinking which may face

[1] Address to the SID World Conference, Ottawa, May 1971.

114

the storm more effectively. First, at the intellectual level, a substantial proportion of influential economists have swung round to a priority emphasis on sustained agricultural development, directly affecting incomes and, less directly, employment of the massive numbers of the rural poor. It is interesting that economists have been influenced to this change of heart mainly by the employment problem, not by the macro-analysis of growth based on Western experience, which dominated thinking for too long. But can it be done? At least much more money for technical research has been poured in by the Foundations and now by other donors, to evolve a new agricultural technology, exemplified in the Green Revolution. But technology is not a sufficient answer : to raise the whole level of small-scale farming, with increasing pressure of population on land, requires an investment, an administrative effort, and a skill in fostering suitable institutions, the nature and scale of which has still not been firmly faced.

The prospects for an attack on unemployment and on poverty can only be regarded with even the smallest gleam of hope if the detailed approach to developing societies is radically changed. Particularly in countries with a 70%/30% rural/urban distribution of population, self-employment (in farming, in small services, in trading, in leading small units of craft production); seasonal and casual employment; and more regular wage-employment, partly on farms but mainly in small constructional, distributive, transport, service, processing, and even small manufacturing units in the rural areas, will have to provide a livelihood for the increasing numbers. This wide-spread addition to livelihoods in the only sector of the economy which is *large* enough to absorb the population growth must largely depend upon the local multiplier effect of sharply increased farm incomes from intensive and more specialised production. Specialisation is needed to ensure an increased domestic market for increased agricultural output. There is much evidence of under-used factory capacity which could meet increased demand from the rural population and help to absorb unemployed labour.

This approach is radically new, because many of the types of livelihood have been precisely those which have largely escaped the statistics and therefore been partially neglected by most macro-economists. Alongside a new attention to this untidy, ill-recorded, un-projectised, but organically vital sector there would have to be changes in central policy (as to urban wage-rates, and exchange and fiscal policies favouring capital-intensive technology and imported consumption goods) which would give a fair wind to endogenous and more labour-intensive activity.

At present the situation and attitudes of donor countries are not by any means entirely favourable to such a programme. One major strand of self-interested thinking, sharpened by balance of payments problems in the USA and by acute competition to export developed-country manufactures (Japan, West Germany), is the suggestion that private investment in LDCs, by giving them 'management skills' and higher productivity in the modern sector, can be substituted for at least part of an aid programme suited to their needs. Unfortunately, developed countries do not easily offer (they have long forgotten) the kind of management skill and technology appropriate for a 10-acre farming economy, craft production, petty trading, and construction with local materials in a tropical climate. Higher productivity in the capital-intensive sector, while it may increase monetary GNP, will assuredly do little to cure unemployment, as indeed we have discovered, from time to time, in the high-wage economies of the West.

We do live, willy nilly, in one economic world, naturally dominated by the concepts, interests and economic pattern of the richest and most powerful countries. Wage-inflation, high prices, an export drive for Western capital and consumption goods, and a present danger of relapse into protectionist blocs, provides about the worst possible 'fit' with the needs of developing countries, pressing upon them just those policies and temptations which have in part led to their present employment predicament. This is not, of course, a sinister conspiracy forced upon unwilling victims. The leaders of many LDCs have themselves set the pace for Westernisation, sometimes even against Western advice.

Nor will a concentration on the least developed twenty-five countries, now envisaged by the UN, go far to avert the storm. It leaves out by far the biggest mass of the poor – for example, in the Indian subcontinent and Indonesia. If there are to be criteria for the application of special effort, they must guide it to the central objective, not to the more easily handled periphery.

As the LDC populations grow towards 5 billions out of a world total of 6½ billions, we have to reassess far more carefully the exact nature of the contribution to their real needs which the small rich world can make. Some parts of our knowledge can be of immense service, including those parts of our technology which are adaptable to their own situation. But it is useless to continue exporting other parts which grew from and depend upon resource endowments and factor prices which are grossly unsuited to that situation. This does not apply only to wages and capital intensity. Highly complex planning and administrative systems, educational volume and structure, labour legislation or social security systems also reflect a wholly different social economy.

116

Indeed, if one may anticipate and greatly sharpen the choices which lie ahead, there seem to be two main, and contrasting, strategies for development which the future holds. The first is a continuation of the process of attempted 'gleichgeschaltung' of LDC economies to the pattern of our own. Through the process of private capital investment, through multinational companies, through the patterning of institutions – Trade Unions, Local Government, Co-operatives, Universities, bureaucracy – on modern Western lines, there might be a more marked absorption, a re-colonisation, of LDC economies as outlying components of the dominant industrial powers. There is at present the proposal to 'associate' many more countries, in Africa, the Caribbean and the Near East, to the European Economic Community. Perhaps when the Treaty of Rome was signed, when France's African possessions were described as 'France Outremer', there was some logic in this. Now, when the LDCs concerned are independent nations, what is the logic, unless it be the logic of economic re-colonisation, in this association of a quite arbitrary selection of nations – arbitrary, that is, unless their common colonial past is still a valid principle of selection? Even this doubtful criterion is not fully applied, since Asia is excluded. Is this because Africa and small economies and islands are felt to have less chance of independent survival than the Asian group? Obviously, there are ties and obligations between European metropolitan countries and their erstwhile dependencies. But these would seem more naturally expressed in bilateral relations than through a trading community formed for quite other basic reasons. There are global systems – UNCTAD, GATT – for regulating trade preferences and tariffs. Let it not be implied that 're-colonisation' implies a deliberate or sinister motive in Europe. Many developing countries see short-term advantage in association with the EEC, or indeed a necessity to join if their competitors do. It is simply that, on both sides, the gradual inclusion of LDC economies within a Western system represents, perhaps half-consciously, a belief that this is the only way forward. Would it repeat, as well as the benefits, the bitterly criticised distortions of the old colonial system?

The second strategy is as yet only struggling to be born. It consists essentially in a far clearer and more reasoned recognition that developing countries must find and pursue a course of development which reflects their own capacities and style: must harness a far greater proportion of their own potential energies through springs and tributaries and streams of action far more widely spread across the whole landscape of their people. Professor Pajestka, in a thoughtful paper from the UN Centre for Economic and Social Information[1], has emphasised that 'development' is social and economic change,

[1] Joseph Pajestka, 'The Social Dimensions of Development', Executive Briefing Paper No. 3, UN, New York, 1970.

117

and therefore essentially internal. LDCs must 'fully assume responsibility for their own modernisation, relying on their own strength and concentrating on increasing their own efficiency . . . . The scope of undertakings resulting from a development policy, which also means the range of active socio-economic changes, must cover the entire economy and the entire society.' He contrasts this development strategy with one of the macro-economic models which have been so much used in the past, which lead to 'the conclusion that the major part of the population of developing countries cannot even dream of reaching – by the end of the century or even later – levels comparable in any degree to the present levels of developed countries'. Such projections are in any case making wrong assumptions about what is desirable : 'It is in no way justified to insist on an increase of . . . material goods and services on a 30-fold or even 10-fold scale, in order to create conditions conducive to a physically wholesome and spiritually creative development for man on a mass scale and to produce an environment likely to prevent him feeling like a pariah in our contemporary world. . . . This sort of development is within the grasp of the majority of developing countries and could be achieved within a generation.'

There have been other voices saying such things – Professor Frankel[1], writing twenty years ago :

'. . . different countries have a different language of social action, and possess, and indeed have long exercised, peculiar aptitudes for solving the problems of their own time and place.'

Professor Harry Johnson[2], in 1970 :

'The essence of the development process . . . is a process of social transformation which can only be effected by a myriad of micro-economic changes, not simply by macroeconomic additions of domestic and foreign resources. These changes have to be effected largely, if not exclusively, by the government and citizens of developing countries themselves.'

H.E. Soedjatmoko[3] :

'Economic development . . . is part of a more general process of transformation . . . . Each nation will have to

[1]H. S. Frankel, *The Economic Impact on Underdeveloped Countries,* Blackwell, Oxford, 1952.
[2]Statement to a sub-Committee of the Joint Economic Committee of the Congress, May 1970.
[3]Asian Ecumenical Conference for Development, Tokyo, July 1970 (Development Digest, Vol. IX No. I, Jan. 1971).

develop its own vision of the future, out of the materials of its own history, its own problems, its own natural make-up.'

This second strategy, then, looks to agricultural and rural development, thus hitting at the centre of under-employment, maldistribution of income, and real need. It looks to a greater effort in basic education for the mass of people, very much including adult education. It looks also to industry, and especially to dispersed manufacturing services and trade. It looks (in Professor Pajestka's words) to 'economic efficiency' achieved by internal socio-economic change.

By no means does such a strategy exclude aid from the developed world. Although I have deliberately sharpened the contrast between a Westernising re-colonisation and a development of indigenous potential in an endogenous socio-economic style, it would be wrong to imply that aid has always been misguided, that tested methods of economic appraisal are inapplicable, that the less dramatic but constant flow of technical assistance and aid to infrastructure has not been of great value. It does imply a more sensitive recognition of different styles of growth; aid to infrastructure which does not prescribe too closely the activities and institutions which are thus supported; aid which enables rather than aid which seeks to shape. It should mean aid which covers local costs and programmes more generously, which is untied, not only to physical purchases from the donor but (even more important) to his institutional, economic and administrative shibboleths. It should mean a sharper distinction between aid which is designed 100% for the recipient's needs and purposes and aid which is mainly commercial export business for the donor.

Finally, it would be absurd to assume, or tacitly imply, that the developed world itself is set on a steady course of ever greater affluence in physical consumption. There are mounting signs of scientific, psychological and moral concern and rejection among the rich nations. The exponential curves of rising resource use and of rising pollution, on a planet with finite limits both of resources and, especially, of ecological viability, are one cause of scientific disquiet. The falling quality of life in some respects (pollution, noise, overcrowding, the spreading concrete jungle, lack of dignity, participation or satisfaction in many forms of work) exerts increasing psychological stress. Only in the last year or two could letters to *The Times* have referred to 'the Frankenstein of growth'[1], or leading articles appeared under the title 'Can we afford to be Rich?'. There is a rising moral

[1]But we should remember that J. K. Galbraith published *The Affluent Society* as long ago as 1958.

rejection, especially among young people, of the purposes, values, and bureaucratic ruthlessness of the acquisitive and affluent society.

Among some of those concerned with overseas development this attack on 'growth'[1] spells danger. If the developed countries should cease to 'grow', *sensu economico,* would this not result in an even greater deceleration in developing countries, as the volume of world trade declined? So recent history seems to show. Thus Mr. Philippe de Seynes, Under-Secretary General for Economic and Social Affairs, in a Statement to the Second Committee of the General Assembly of the United Nations (29 September 1971), makes a surprisingly impassioned defence of 'growth' :

> 'It is necessary to reaffirm that growth continues to be the mainspring of social progress and, in a sense, its guardian angel.
> ' . . . The future of developing countries is inextricably linked with the growth of industrial countries. . . . *No doubt new approaches may be developed that will somewhat reduce dependence on industrial markets, encourage trade between countries of the Third World and regional integration and stimulate new schemes for development based more directly on national effort.* Nevertheless, the fundamental interaction, the secular correlation, of which there is ample evidence, between the progress of the Third World and the growth of industrial countries is still an essential factor. Nothing in the present or foreseeable organisation of relations on this planet justifies the belief that some new dynamic can take the place of this beneficent correlation . . . There is no scientifically valid judgment on the capacity of the biosphere or the exhaustion of natural resources that would at this point justify us in saying that growth must be halted or slowed down . . . . '

These are strong words, and brave words, issued from a country accounting for 40% of the world's natural resource use, in which Lake Erie is already 'dead' from pollution, and in which a Court can order the closing down of a number of factories owing to imminent risk of dangerous accumulation of atmospheric pollution in the air above New York (November 1971). No doubt the scientific evidence will be further examined in the Stockholm Conference on the Environment this summer. Nevertheless, in view of existing statements by responsible scientists, it might be wise to accelerate the 'new

[1] It is, in my view, unfortunate that 'growth', in economic literature, is used in the narrow meaning of 'growth of GNP', and 'development' for wider social growth. I would prefer 'growth' in a wide, organic sense, and 'development' for the efforts of economic planners.

120

approaches' which I have italicised in Mr. de Seynes's statement, and which accord closely with the argument of this chapter.

It might be wise, also, to define more closely what 'growth' is to mean. If, in both developed and developing countries, it is an ever-increasing output of physical objects, power, etc., that is one thing. But if it might mean in developed countries a change of emphasis from quantity to quality of life, a decreasing concentration on objects of consumption, an increasing emphasis on less material, though costly, values – quiet, clean air and water, privacy, rewarding work; then the effects of 'slowing down' material growth might not be so destructive to the future of developing countries, particularly if they in turn were concerned to build upon their own resources the type of development which Professor Pajestka has sketched. The exporters of minerals (both metal and oil) in LDCs might indeed feel the pinch if physical growth slowed down. But there is no reason why a slightly less compulsive consumption of physical products in the industrial world should reduce some of the vital exports of tropical countries – tea, coffee, sugar, vegetable oils, bananas and other fruits, or even Indian textiles. Much of the debris and pollution in industrial countries – metal, chemical and plastic wastes, automobile fumes – comes from their own internal production.

A year of the Second Development Decade has already passed – a year in which 13m people will have been added to India's population. We have, even in terms of food production, a very short breathing space (perhaps 20 years if tremendous efforts are made) before population growth inexorably gains on food production. We have probably even less time before poverty, maldistribution of income, unemployment and overcrowding result in even worse outbreaks of violence. It may seem inappropriate to be speculating on longer and more complex issues when the hard, practical tasks, and the need for renewed effort, are so vivid and urgent. But surely the experience of the last 20 years shows that we need, not only to try harder, but to think harder and to think freshly. We need a new formulation of the nature of development, and especially of ways to use the wasted human potential in developing countries. We need a greater historical sense of the ways in which human communities have built for themselves a modest prosperity in earlier periods, long before the present and perhaps temporary pattern of industrial affluence came to dominate men's minds and to divide the world in such unequal groups. There are signs of fresh thinking, still tentative, but gaining strength. If, by reformulation, we can find a way forward in which our efforts are less wastefully, more aptly applied, the gain is great. Subject to one great threat, human knowledge and good purpose are well able to meet the future, however stormy it may seem. The threat lies in the growth of human numbers, which could yet defeat all that the best of knowledge and purpose can devise.

Table A.1 Regional Distribution of British Bilateral Aid, 1966-1969 (annual average) and 1970[1]

£'000

Recipient	Gross Aid				Net Aid[2]				Net as % of Gross	
	1966-69	%	1970	%	1966-69	%	1970	%	1966-69	1970
Europe and Middle East										
Commonwealth	11,030	6·0	8,764	4·5	10,315	8·1	8,003	5·6	93·5	91·3
Non-Commonwealth	10,395	5·7	7,818	4·0	7,860	6·2	5,699	4·0	75·6	72·9
Africa										
Commonwealth	63,451	34·6	58,669	30·3	45,799	36·1	36,559	25·7	72·2	62·3
Non-Commonwealth	1,716	0·9	2,632	1·4	974	0·8	1,615	1·1	56·8	61·4
Asia										
Commonwealth	64,580	35·3	74,713	38·5	36,371	28·7	51,527	36·2	56·3	69·0
Non-Commonwealth	4,465	2·4	6,319	3·3	4,384	3·5	5,401	3·8	98·2	85·5
Central America & Caribbean										
Commonwealth	11,089	6·1	14,759	7·6	8,596	6·8	11,647	8·2	77·5	78·9
Non-Commonwealth	157	0·1	348	0·2	157	0·1	348	0·2	100·0	100·0
South America										
Commonwealth	2,196	1·2	3,566	1·8	881	0·7	2,172	1·5	40·1	60·9
Non-Commonwealth	2,891	1·6	1,670	0·9	-2,117	-1·7	-2,603	-1·8	—	—
Oceania										
Commonwealth	5,411	3·0	8,299	4·3	5,220	4·1	8,112	5·7	96·5	97·8
Other	4,913	2·7	10,728	5·5	6,742	5·3	10,771	7·5		
CDC Adjustment	880	0·5	-4,358	-2·2	1,595	1·3	3,255	2·3		
Total	183,174	100·0	193,927	100·0	126,776	100·0	142,504	100·0	69·2	73·5

Notes: 1. Includes CDC investment since no breakdown of Exchequer advances is available by country. The adjustment at the bottom of the table brings the grand total back to the official figure for the bilateral aid programme.
2. Net of amortisation and interest.

Source: *British Aid Statistics 1966 to 1970*, HMSO, 1971, Table 11.

Table A.2 Largest Recipients of British Bilateral Aid, 1966-1969 (annual average) and 1970

Recipient	Ranking on Total 1966-70 Receipts Gross	Ranking on Total 1966-70 Receipts Net	Gross Aid £'000 1966-69	Gross Aid £'000 1970	Net Aid¹ £'000 1966-69	Net Aid¹ £'000 1970	Net as % of Gross 1966-69	Net as % of Gross 1970	Net Aid per Head of Recipient Population² (£) 1966-69	Net Aid per Head of Recipient Population² (£) 1970	Net Aid per Head as % of Recipient's GNP per Head³ 1966-69	Net Aid per Head as % of Recipient's GNP per Head³ 1970
Aden/S. Arabia	14	10	4,596	112	4,426	112	96·3	100·0	··	3·97	··	··
Botswana	10	7	5,232	2,795	4,951	2,496	94·6	89·3	7·87	18·90	6·7	8·6
Br. Honduras	23	20	1,794	2,306	1,719	2,211	95·8	95·9	14·69	4·39	··	0·4
Ceylon	13	9	3,957	4,543	3,486	4,274	88·1	94·0	0·28	0·61	0·4	2·7
Fiji	25	22	1,690	2,398	1,508	2,222	89·2	92·7	2·98	2·99	1·8	0·8
Ghana	16	11	3,259	5,488	2,898	5,067	88·9	92·3	0·35	0·06	0·4	2·1
Guyana	19	25	2,196	3,566	881	2,172	40·1	60·9	1·21	0·02	0·9	0·1
India	1	1	38,803	44,780	18,089	29,158	46·6	65·1	0·03	0·01	0·1	—
Indonesia	26	23	1,027	2,659	1,027	2,631	100·0	98·9	0·01	0·06	—	—
Iran	28	27	1,255	615	1,099	144	87·6	23·4	0·04	-0·17	—	
Jamaica	20	28	2,524	1,811	971	-309	38·4	—	0·52	0·48	0·2	0·4
Jordan	24	19	2,084	1,069	2,084	1,069	100·0	100·0	0·93	0·58	0·8	1·1
Kenya	2	4	10,850	11,099	6,706	6,357	61·8	57·3	0·62	0·32	1·1	0·7
Laos	27	24	1,453	926	1,453	926	100·0	100·0	0·50	0·66	1·1	··
Lesotho	11	13	3,982	653	3,943	612	99·0	93·7	4·24	1·50	··	0·2
Malawi	4	3	8,130	7,709	7,304	6,602	89·8	85·6	1·66	0·30	0·2	7·0
Malaysia	7	15	5,515	6,538	2,662	3,172	48·3	48·5	0·25	20·83	5·6	1·7
Malta	6	5	5,629	7,338	5,304	6,729	94·2	91·7	16·42	1·65	2·5	··
Mauritius	22	21	2,275	1,693	1,938	1,315	85·2	77·7	2·43	0·10	··	0·1
Nigeria	5	12	6,049	11,030	2,589	6,211	42·8	56·3	0·04	0·06	0·1	1·1
Pakistan	3	2	10,844	10,618	7,182	7,420	66·2	69·9	0·06	3·77	0·3	23·9
Singapore	17	14	2,125	7,878	1,897	7,613	89·2	96·6	0·94	20·87	16·2	··
Solomon Is.	18	17	2,249	3,318	2,249	3,318	100·0	100·0	14·14	0·01	0·1	1·6
Sudan	29	29	860	698	477	91	55·5	13·0	0·03	1·20	0·3	0·1
Swaziland	15	18	4,076	3,129	2,509	490	61·6	15·7	6·12	0·50	8·2	0·1
Tanzania	21	26	2,298	2,030	1,105	606	48·1	29·9	0·09	0·11	0·1	0·6
Turkey	8	6	5,260	5,178	4,917	3,698	93·5	71·4	0·14	0·26	0·1	0·1
Uganda	12	16	4,390	4,352	2,772	2,458	63·1	56·5	0·29	0·48	0·6	0·6
Zambia	9	8	5,749	2,569	5,065	1,919	88·1	74·7	1·26		1·0	0·4
Total			150,151	158,898	103,211	110,784	68·7	69·7				
World Total			183,174	193,927	126,776	142,504	69·2	73·5				
Countries above as % of World Total			82·0	81·9	81·4	77·7						

Notes: 1. Net of amortisation and interest.
2. Using IBRD population estimates for mid-1969.
3. Using IBRD estimates of GNP per head in 1969. Converted from Dollars at $2.4 = £1.

Sources: *British Aid Statistics.*
World Bank Atlas, 1971.

.. Not available.

Table A.3 Largest Recipients of British Bilateral Aid, 1966-1969 (annual average) and 1970: Functional Breakdown

Recipient	Financial Aid				Grants		Technical Assistance							
	Net ODA Loans (net of amortisation and interest)		CDC investments (net of amortisation and interest)				Technical assistance grants		British personnel sent (numbers leaving Britain, excluding volunteers)		Volunteers sent (during British fiscal year)		Students and Trainees (numbers arriving in Britain)	
	1966-69	1970	1966-69	1970	1966-69	1970	1966-69	1970	1966-69	1970	1966-69	1970	1966-69	1970
Aden/S. Arabia	4,425	112	—	—	4,132	4	457	108	34	—	—	—	31	28
Botswana	5,008	2,651	-57	-155	4,368	1,856	427	577	70	67	31	28	18	32
Br. Honduras	1,729	2,225	-10	-14	1,485	655	185	326	13	11	27	21	26	264
Ceylon	3,486	4,274	—	—	—	956	267	376	18	18	12	20	155	69
Fiji	1,492	2,223	16	-1	994	1,467	665	922	42	51	9	9	42	267
Ghana	2,780	4,967	118	100	—	—	600	933	69	54	102	44	182	70
Guyana	596	635	285	1,537	880	100	162	234	19	20	25	7	54	648
India	18,089	29,158	—	—	—	1,697	769	867	25	26	81	62	402	79
Indonesia	1,027	2,631	—	—	233	37	37	161	1	2	—	14	17	101
Iran	1,099	144	—	—	—	—	324	469	17	26	6	—	113	76
Jamaica	169	-856	802	-547	48	—	294	383	22	36	39	37	74	63
Jordan	2,084	1,069	—	—	1,072	586	157	178	10	4	9	—	78	177
Kenya	6,309	6,448	397	-91	697	100	3,307	3,271	325	193	91	68	140	7
Laos	1,453	926	—	—	1,281	748	172	178	5	4	7	10	2	18
Lesotho	3,943	612	—	—	3,556	348	290	249	36	7	22	14	41	120
Malawi	7,305	7,110	-1[1]	-508[1]	3,631	2,624	1,518	1,685	148	166	65	65	103	265
Malaysia	3,330	4,456	-668	-1,284	2,213	56	1,614	1,435	59	37	43	13	167	39
Malta	5,304	6,729	—	—	4,387	7,261	59	77	14	36	7	2	51	87
Mauritius	1,835	1,353	103	-38	1,068	698	191	194	13	13	6	5	35	499
Nigeria	2,963	6,010	-374	201	1,176	2,847	1,778	1,499	127	163	100	157	337	338
Pakistan	7,182	7,420	—	—	—	479	847	807	11	24	34	29	239	92
Singapore	1,533	6,536	364	1,077	706	1,494	193	287	10	19	9	11	71	19
Solomon Is.	2,242	3,290	7	28	1,641	2,075	596	1,096	36	49	25	27	11	187
Sudan	477	91	—	—	64	—	250	472	13	6	20	33	163	34
Swaziland	3,066	1,747	-557	-1,257	1,918	839	339	452	44	57	18	30	37	58
Tanzania	1,671	1,211	-566	-605	225	—	1,550	1,792	81	8	85	36	67	162
Turkey	4,917	3,698	—	—	—	—	406	251	7	12	4	1	144	206
Uganda	2,844	2,706	-72	-248	—	—	2,267	2,025	287	163	74	45	180	92
Zambia	1,328	2,292	3,737[1]	-373[1]	234	39	3,592	2,523	691	664	67	66	104	—
Total	99,686	111,868	3,524	-2,178	36,009	26,966	23,313	23,827	2,247	1,936	1,020	854	3,084	4,097
World Total	122,986	143,354	3,790	-850	54,085	39,737	37,230	45,572	2,863	2,669	1,611	1,322	5,819	7,513
Countries above as % of World Total	81.1	78.0	93.0	—	66.5	67.9	62.6	52.3	78.5	72.5	63.3	64.6	53.0	54.5

Notes: 1. Excludes joint amortisation and interest payments for Malawi, Rhodesia and Zambia, of £1,059,000 in 1966-69 (average) and £1,167,000 in 1970.
Source: *British Aid Statistics.*

125

Table A.4   British Multilateral Aid, 1966-1969 and 1970
£m

	Annual Average 1966-69	1970
Contributions towards financial aid		
International Bank for Reconstruction and Development (IBRD)	—	1·4
International Development Association (IDA)	14·2	6·4
Asian Development Bank (ADB)	0·8	0·6
Caribbean Development Bank (CDB)	—	0·4
World Food Programme (WFP)	1·1	2·2
UN Refugee Programmes	1·8	2·0
Other	†	†
Total	17·9	13·0
Contributions towards technical assistance		
United Nations Development Programme (UNDP)	4·8	5·9
United Nations International Children's Emergency Fund (UNICEF)	0·5	0·6
Other UN Agencies	0·1	0·2
Other	†	0·2
Total	5·4	6·8
Total UK Multilateral Aid	23·3	19·8
as a percentage of gross aid	11·3%	9·2%

Note: † Less than £50,000.
Source: *British Aid Statistics 1966–1970*, HMSO, 1971, Tables 4 and 9.

Table A. 5   World Exports by Area of Origin, 1970¹

	Value $m	% of World Total
Developed Countries		
North America	60,088	19·4
EEC	88,686	28·6
Britain	19,351	6·2
EFTA (other than Britain)	23,816	7·7
Other Industrial W. Europe	4,200	1·4
USSR and E. Europe	30,909	10·0
S. Africa, New Zealand, Australia	8,470	2·7
Japan	19,333	6·2
Total	**254,853**	**82·1**
Developing Countries		
Brazil, Argentina, Mexico	5,912	1·9
Other Latin America & Caribbean	9,638	3·1
European LDCs	3,253	1·1
Israel	781	0·3
Arab Middle East & N. Africa	14,289	4·6
Other Africa	7,742	2·5
Hong Kong, Taiwan, Singapore, S. Korea	6,331	2·0
India, Pakistan, Indonesia	3,491	1·1
Other S. & E. Asia²	4,178	1·4
Total	**55,615**	**17·9**
World Total	**310,468**	**100·0**

Notes: 1. Geographical areas are defined as follows:
North America: Canada, United States.
EFTA (other than UK): Austria, Denmark, Finland, Norway, Portugal, Sweden, Switzerland.
Other Industrial West Europe: Greece, Iceland, Ireland, Spain.
USSR and E. Europe: Albania, Bulgaria, Czechoslovakia, E. Germany, Hungary, Poland, Romania, USSR.
Other Latin America and Caribbean: Bolivia, Chile, Colombia, Costa Rica, Cuba, Dominican Republic, Ecuador, El Salvador, Guatemala, Haiti, Honduras, Nicaragua, Panama, Paraguay, Peru, Venezuela, Uruguay, West Indies.
European LDCs: Cyprus, Gibraltar, Malta, Turkey, Yugoslavia.
Arab Middle East and North Africa: Gulf States, Iran, Iraq, Jordan, Lebanon, Saudi Arabia, Syria, UAR, Yemen, Algeria, Libya, Morocco, Tunisia.
Other Africa: All Africa, including Malagasy Republic, except South Africa, Algeria, Libya, Morocco, Tunisia, UAR.
Other S. & E. Asia: Afghanistan, Brunei, Burma, Cambodia, Ceylon, China, N. Korea, Laos, Macao, Malaysia, Nepal, Philippines, Ryukyu Is., Thailand, N. Vietnam, S. Vietnam.
2. Trade among Asian Communist countries is excluded.
Source: *International Financial Statistics*, IMF, June 1971.
International Trade, GATT, 1970.

126

Table A.6 Network of International Trade: Exports, 1960 and 1968 $ million f.o.b.

Origin / Destination	Year	N. America	EEC	UK	EFTA (other than Britain)	Other Industrial W. Europe	USSR and E. Europe	SA, NZ, Australia	Japan	Total Developed Countries	Brazil, Argentina Mexico	Other Latin America and Caribbean
North America	1960	6,823	3,924	2,359	1,076	342	227	925	1,527	17,203	1,680	2,338
	1968	16,602	6,847	3,424	1,774	839	344	1,713	3,517	35,060	2,512	3,308
EEC	1960	2,532	10,250	1,760	5,111	590	992	608	209	22,052	770	982
	1968	6,382	28,930	3,130	8,515	1,962	2,373	1,186	637	53,115	1,072	1,535
Britain (UK)	1960	1,574	1,573	—	1,244	478	270	1,512	82	6,733	229	571
	1968	2,818	3,099	—	2,121	1,045	548	1,647	236	11,514	266	557
EFTA (other than Britain)	1960	763	3,134	1,424	1,484	174	613	199	54	7,845	270	238
	1968	1,655	5,195	2,554	3,965	502	1,110	316	205	15,502	372	375
Other Industrial West Europe	1960	151	384	471	103	7	80	8	16	1,220	32	33
	1968	461	760	746	228	27	159	26	27	2,434	83	172
USSR and East Europe	1960	94	1,173	388	662	59	8,086	10	80	10,552	122	87
	1968	269	1,910	654	992	200	15,200	31	51	19,772	102	592
South Africa, New Zealand, Australia	1960	383	688	1,382	59	16	87	206	381	3,202	24	18
	1968	891	889	1,624	72	60	95	319	1,172	5,122	23	55
Japan	1960	1,227	175	121	111	59	64	225	—	1,982	92	186
	1968	4,479	687	365	417	161	233	685	—	7,027	251	445
Total Developed Countries	**1960**	**13,547**	**21,301**	**7,905**	**9,850**	**1,725**	**10,419**	**3,693**	**2,349**	**70,789**	**3,219**	**4,453**
	1968	**33,557**	**48,317**	**12,497**	**18,084**	**4,796**	**20,062**	**5,923**	**6,310**	**149,546**	**4,681**	**7,039**
Brazil, Argentina, Mexico	1960	1,137	726	298	157	37	132	16	116	2,619	142	158
	1968	1,537	1,046	192	214	158	176	17	159	3,499	293	359
Other Latin America and Caribbean	1960	3,140	941	711	197	62	127	24	101	5,303	293	1,111
	1968	3,726	1,392	753	366	208	345	22	578	7,390	270	1,343

Origin / Destination		N. America	EEC	UK	EFTA (other than Britain)	Other Industrial W. Europe	USSR and E. Europe	SA, NZ, Australia	Japan	Total Developed Countries	Brazil, Argentina Mexico	Other Latin America and Caribbean
European LDCs	1960	100	276	98	75	32	222	1	3	807	8	3
	1968	171	554	141	155	63	533	2	19	1,638	3	16
Israel	1960	32	62	36	25	4	4	3	2	168	2	2
	1968	132	169	71	59	16	19	10	24	500	5	4
Arab Middle East and N. Africa	1960	400	2,146	805	159	166	290	210	384	4,560	48	16
	1968	346	4,877	1,479	433	502	455	312	1,596	10,000	160	56
Other Africa	1960	476	1,517	896	183	24	79	130	61	3,366	4	7
	1968	648	2,287	911	333	97	118	70	326	4,790	26	20
Hong Kong, Taiwan, Singapore, S. Korea	1960	268	150	205	39	14	51	110	174	1,011	30	30
	1968	1,267	243	303	73	6	—	109	379	2,380	16	40
India, Pakistan, Indonesia	1960	480	259	527	22	22	147	122	134	1,713	18	31
	1968	602	414	383	61	27	370	132	479	2,468	5	15
Other South and East Asia	1960	525	612	375	83	22	1,468	154	494	3,733	21	31
	1968	817	603	278	128	39	507	139	1,033	3,544	18	17
Total Developing Countries	**1960**	**6,558**	**6,689**	**3,951**	**940**	**383**	**2,520**	**770**	**1,469**	**23,280**	**566**	**1,389**
	1968	**9,246**	**11,585**	**4,511**	**1,822**	**1,116**	**2,523**	**813**	**4,593**	**36,209**	**796**	**1,870**
TOTAL (a) $ million	**1960**	**20,105**	**27,990**	**11,856**	**10,790**	**2,108**	**12,939**	**4,463**	**3,818**	**94,069**	**3,785**	**5,342**
	1968	**42,803**	**59,902**	**17,008**	**19,906**	**5,912**	**22,585**	**6,736**	**10,903**	**185,755**	**5,477**	**8,909**
(b) % of World Total	**1960**	**15·6**	**21·7**	**9·2**	**8·3**	**1·6**	**10·0**	**3·5**	**3·0**	**73·0**	**2·9**	**4·5**
	1968	**18·2**	**25·5**	**7·2**	**8·5**	**2·5**	**9·6**	**2·9**	**4·6**	**79·0**	**2·3**	**3·8**

Table A.6 Network of International Trade: Exports, 1960 and 1968

$ million f.o.b.

Origin	Destination	European LDCs	Israel	Arab Middle East and N. Africa	Other Africa	Hong Kong, Taiwan, Singapore, S. Korea	India, Pakistan, Indonesia	Other S. & E. Asia	Total Developing Countries	Residual	TOTAL (a) $m	TOTAL (b) % of World Total
North America	1960	235	133	648	218	459	950	536	7,197	1,681	26,081	20·2
	1968	388	288	1,142	489	1,350	1,323	1,301	12,101	60	47,221	20·1
EEC	1960	558	147	2,456	1,151	202	600	597	7,463	228	29,743	23·1
	1968	1,133	346	2,696	1,871	429	643	939	10,664	474	64,253	27·3
Britain (UK)	1960	169	46	504	812	221	592	401	3,545	19	10,297	8·0
	1968	259	211	720	771	308	303	407	3,802	31	15,347	6·5
EFTA (other than Britain)	1960	121	34	219	224	59	118	115	1,398	16	9,259	7·2
	1968	232	87	368	438	156	118	209	2,355	44	17,901	7·6
Other Industrial West Europe	1960	19	3	27	26	1	6	6	153	48	1,421	1·1
	1968	38	6	108	27	3	4	9	450	52	2,936	1·3
USSR and East Europe	1960	246	3	267	31	—	128	1,416	2,300	361	13,213	10·3
	1968	559	18	574	127	7	349	999	3,327	4	23,103	9·8
South Africa, New Zealand, Australia	1960	24	5	48	245	72	65	134	635	296	4,133	3·2
	1968	34	8	50	378	204	66	347	1,165	245	6,532	2·7
Japan	1960	18	3	164	263	445	278	593	2,042	31	4,055	3·2
	1968	50	14	485	680	1,751	402	1,785	5,863	76	12,966	5·5
Total Developed Countries	1960	1,390	374	4,333	2,970	1,459	2,737	3,798	24,733	2,680	98,202	76·2˙
	1968	2,693	978	6,143	4,781	4,208	3,208	5,996	39,727	986	190,259	80·9
Brazil, Argentina, Mexico	1960	12	3	16	2	6	8	12	359	137	3,115	2·4
	1968	20	15	45	17	25	4	8	786	219	4,504	1·9
Other Latin America and Caribbean	1960	16	3	47	63	4	7	54	1,598	103	7,004	5·4
	1968	25	7	31	0	37	7	9	1,729	253	9,372	4·0

129

Origin / Destination		European LDCs	Israel	Arab Middle East and N. Africa	Other Africa	Hong Kong, Taiwan, Singapore, S. Korea	India, Pakistan, Indonesia	Other S. & E. Asia	Total Developing Countries	Residual	TOTAL (a) $m	TOTAL (b) % of World Total
European LDCs	1960	10	12	60	12	—	21	11	137	7	951	0·7
	1968	13	16	104	6	0	57	12	227	12	1,877	0·8
Israel	1960	15	—	0	9	8	—	3	39	8	215	0·2
	1968	19	—	17	23	31	—	8	107	34	641	0·3
Arab Middle East and N. Africa	1960	68	0	383	124	57	223	90	1,009	94	5,663	4·4
	1968	121	2	437	172	160	272	129	1,509	8	11,517	4·9
Other Africa	1960	12	12	90	125	13	109	31	403	129	3,898	3·0
	1968	26	21	87	286	33	65	52	616	112	5,518	2·4
Hong Kong, Taiwan, Singapore, S. Korea	1960	8	1	49	41	83	95	648	985	23	2,019	1·6
	1968	1	8	57	90	301	96	302	911	24	3,315	1·4
India, Pakistan, Indonesia	1960	16	0	108	75	245	67	271	831	20	2,564	2·0
	1968	38	0	208	108	151	10	195	730	2	3,200	1·4
Other South and East Asia	1960	24	2	68	26	680	255	367	1,474	76	5,283	4·1
	1968	18	1	136	86	603	181	225	1,285	52	4,881	2·1
Total Developing Countries	1960	181	33	821	477	1,096	785	1,487	6,835	597	30,712	23·8
	1968	281	70	1,122	788	1,341	692	940	7,900	716	44,825	19·1
TOTAL (a) $ million	1960	1,571	407	5,154	3,447	2,555	3,522	5,285	31,568	3,277	128,914	100·0
	1968	2,974	1,048	7,265	5,569	5,549	3,900	6,936	47,627	1,702	235,084	100·0
(b) % of World Total	1960	1·2	0·3	4·0	2·7	2·0	2·7	4·1	24·5	2·5	100·0	100·0
	1968	1·2	0·5	3·1	2·4	2·4	1·7	3·0	20·3	0·7	100·0	100·0

Notes: 1. For definition of geographical areas, see Table A.5, note 1.
2. Trade among Asian communist countries is excluded.

Sources: *Direction of Trade, 1960–64 and 1964–68*, International Monetary Fund.
International Trade, 1968, GATT.

Appendix B General Preference Schemes: Offers made by Developed Countries

Country	Date of Operation 1	Period of Operation 2	Coverage 3
United Kingdom	1.1.72	1.1.72–1.1.74 (unification with EEC System by 1974)	All BTN[2] 25–99 except those in Col. 4 Over 140 PAG items in BTN 1–24
European Community	1.7.71	1.7.71–1.1.74	All BTN 25–99 "without exception" (but see Col. 4) Selected items in BTN 1–24 (N.B. Common Agricultural Policy variable levies still stand)
United States	Not decided	Not decided	All manufactures and semimanufactures except (Col. 4) 100 tariff items of industrial primary products 180 tariff items of PAGs
Japan	1.8.71		All 25–99 except (Col. 4). "A range" of PAGs
Nordic Countries (Sweden, Norway, Denmark, Finland)	1.10.71 (Norway) 1.1.72 (Sweden) (Denmark) (Finland)	Till 1974 for Norway and Denmark	All industrial products, including raw materials except (Col. 4) "A range" of PAGs
Austria	1.1.72	..	All manufactures and semimanufactures in 25–99 except (Col. 4)
Switzerland	1.1.72	..	All 25–99 except (Col. 4) Some PAGs
Ireland	1.1.72	..	All manufactures and semimanufactures in 25–99 except (Col. 4)
Canada	..	..	All manufactures and semimanufactures except (Col. 4) Some PAGs
New Zealand	1.1.72	..	"A list" of agricultural and industrial products
Australia	1.1.66	..	Positive lists covering confectionery only in 1–24 and a selection of 25–99
Eastern Europe	1.1.72	..	Not clear, except that Czechoslovakia has cut tariffs on LDC imports by 50%. Hungary has also introduced a scheme

| Exceptions | Depth of Preference | | Safeguard Clauses |
4	Manufactures 5	PAG[1] 6	7
Cotton and competing synthetic textiles Hydrocarbon oils Perfumes Matches and lighters	Duty free entry or Commonwealth preference rate	Duty free entry or Commonwealth preference rate	"Right to withdraw"
Jute and coir products: special negotiation with India, Pakistan Industrial raw materials in 25–99, including metals up to ingot stage	Duty free entry	Partial duty reductions	"Right to withdraw" for PAG: global tariff quotas and country ceilings for manufactures (See Ch. 7)
Cotton, wool and man made fibre textiles; clothing, footwear, petrochemicals, petroleum products All LDCs granting reverse preferences	Duty free entry	Duty free entry	Escape clause, dependent on Tariff Commission hearings
Hydrocarbon oils, leather clothing, silk fabrics, rubber or plastic footwear	50% of duty on textiles, leather goods, toys. Duty free entry for all others	50% on most, but 100% on some	"Right to withdraw" for specific PAGs from specific sources. Quotas (imports from LDCs in 1968 and 10% from all others in most recent year) and country ceilings (50% of quota)
Textiles, tyres, leather, leather clothing, footwear, pottery and china, glassware, cycles and motor cycles, furniture	Duty free entry	Duty free entry	"Right to withdraw"
Cotton textiles, any product bearing variable levies or equalisation charges	30% duty reduction	—	Quotas (LDC imports, over 25% above previous year or for most competitive LDC, over 10% above)
Goods bearing fiscal duties	30% duty reduction	Duty free entry or reductions	"Right to withdraw"
Most textiles, tyres, most leather, footwear, vehicles and parts	One-third duty reduction	—	"Right to withdraw"
(Mainly textiles)	One third cut or to British Preferential rates, whichever lower (B P rate is often zero)	—	"Right to withdraw"
..	To British Preferential rate—which is usually zero	—	"Right to withdraw"
Products competing with Australian industries?	Varying: some duty free, others only partial. Handcraft products (inc. handloom textiles) duty free	—	"Right to withdraw" and quotas on all except handcrafts
Some textiles, footwear, PAGs	Czechoslovakia 50%: others not yet clear	—	

.. Not available.

Notes: 1. PAGs = processed agricultural goods.
2. BTN = Brussels Tariff Nomenclature.
Sources: *Trade and Industry,* HMSO, 24 March 1971.
UNCTAD Documents TD/B/AC.5/24 and 5/34, Addenda 1–10.

Appendix C Developing Countries covered by the British General Preference Scheme[1].

Independent countries

Afghanistan
Algeria
Argentina
Bahrain
Barbados
Bolivia
Botswana
Brazil
Burma
Burundi
Cameroon
Central African Republic
Ceylon
Chad
Chile
Colombia
Congo, Democratic Republic of the
Congo, People's Republic of the
Costa Rica
Cyprus
Dahomey
Dominican Republic
Ecuador
Egypt, Arab Republic of
El Salvador
Equatorial Guinea
Ethiopia
Fiji
Gabon
Gambia, The
Ghana
Guatemala
Guinea
Guyana
Haiti

Honduras
India
Indonesia
Iran
Iraq
Ivory Coast
Jamaica
Jordan
Kenya
Khmer Republic (Cambodia)
Korea, Republic of
Kuwait
Laos
Lebanon
Lesotho
Liberia
Libyan Arab Republic
Madagascar
Malawi
Malaysia
Maldives
Mali
Malta
Mauritania
Mauritius
Mexico
Morocco
Nauru
Nepal
Nicaragua
Niger
Nigeria
Pakistan
Panama
Paraguay
Peru

Philippines
Qatar
Rwanda
Saudi Arabia
Senegal
Sierra Leone
Singapore
Somali Democratic Republic
Sudan
Swaziland
Syria
Tanzania
Thailand
Togo
Tonga
Trinidad and Tobago
Trucial States:
  Abu Dhabi
  Dubai
  Ras-al-Kaimah
  Fujairah
  Ajman
  Sharjah
  Umm-al-Qaiwan
Tunisia
Uganda
Upper Volta
Uruguay
Venezuela
Vietnam, Republic of
Western Samoa
Yemen Arab Republic
Yemen, People's Democratic Republic of
Yugoslavia
Zambia

Dependent territories, associated states and states whose external relations are conducted by third countries

Angola
Antigua
Australian Antarctic Territory

Bahamas
Bermuda
British Antarctic Territory

British Honduras

British Indian Ocean Territory (comprising the Chagos Archipelago, Aldabra, Farquhar and Desroches)

British Solomon Islands Protectorate

Brunei

Cape Verde Islands

Cayman Islands

Christmas Island

Cocos (Keeling) Islands

Corn Islands and Swan Islands

Dominica

Falkland Islands and Dependencies

French Antarctic Territories

French Polynesia

Gibraltar

Gilbert and Ellice Islands Colony

Grenada

Heard Island and McDonald Islands

Hong Kong

Macao

Montserrat

Mozambique

Netherlands Antilles

New Caledonia and Dependencies

New Hebrides Condominium

Norfolk Island

Overseas Territories of New Zealand:
Niue Island, Tokelau Islands, Ross Dependency and the Cook Islands

Pacific Islands administered by the USA:
Guam, American Samoa (comprising Swain Island), Midway Islands, Johnston Island, Sand Island, Baker, Howland and Jarvis Islands, Wake Island and Johnson Atoll and Kingman Reef.
The following mandated islands—the Carolines, the Marinas, and the Marshall Islands.

Papua—New Guinea

Pitcairn

Portuguese Guinea

Portuguese Timor

Prince and Sao Tome Islands

St. Christopher-Nevis-Anguilla

St. Helena (with Ascension and Tristan da Cunha)

St. Lucia

St. Pierre and Miquelon

St. Vincent

Seychelles

Spanish North Africa

Surinam

Territory of New Guinea

Turks and Caicos Islands

Virgin Islands (British)

Virgin Islands (USA)

Wallis and Futuna Islands

Note: 1. The countries listed are also those covered by the EEC GSP, except that Equatorial Guinea, Nauru and Tonga appear to be excluded. In the EEC's 1971 classification, Bahrain, Qatar and the Trucial States have been counted as dependencies. Fiji has not yet been included in the EEC system but is being given consideration, as are Bhutan and Cuba. Malta is excluded but has an Association Agreement with the EEC.

Source: *Trade and Industry*, 23 September 1971, p. 578.

Glossary

AID	Agency for International Development
BTN	Brussels Tariff Nomenclature
CAP	Common Agricultural Policy
CDC	Commonwealth Development Corporation
CSA	Commonwealth Sugar Agreement
DAC	Development Assistance Committee (of OECD)
DOM	Départements d'Outre-Mer (French Overseas Departments)
DTI	Department of Trade and Industry
ECOSOC	Economic and Social Council of the United Nations
EDF	European Development Fund
EEC	European Economic Community
EFTA	European Free Trade Association
EIB	European Investment Bank
FAO	Food and Agriculture Organisation
FCO	Foreign and Commonwealth Office
GATT	General Agreement on Tariffs and Trade
GNP	Gross National Product
GSP	General Scheme of Preferences
IBRD	International Bank for Reconstruction and Development ('World Bank')
IDA	International Development Association
IDB	Inter-American Development Bank
IMF	International Monetary Fund
LDC	less developed country
NEP	New Economic Policy
NNP	Net National Product
ODA	Overseas Development Administration
	official development assistance
ODM	Ministry of Overseas Development
OECD	Organisation for European Co-operation and Development
SDRs	Special Drawing Rights
SID	Society for International Development
UNCTAD	United Nations Conference on Trade and Development
UNDP	United Nations Development Programme
cif	cost, insurance, freight
fob	free on board
mfn	most favoured nation

135

Index

Frankel, Professor H. S. (*The Economic Impact on Underdeveloped Countries*), 122n
French Overseas Departments (DOM), 107
Fukuda, Haruko, 98n

Galbraith, J. K. (*The Affluent Society*), 123n
Geet, Dick van, 11, 77
General Agreement on Tariffs and Trade (GATT), 9, 16, 95
  tariff quota systems, 17, 18
  the 'Kennedy Round', 65
General Preference Schemes (GSPs), 9, 16, 133
  Special Committee on, 17
  British and EEC, 57–8, 95, 108–14, 135, 136
Germany, 25, 31, 32, 98, 110n, 120

Haq, Mahbub ul, 'Employment in the 1970s', 116n, 118
Howe, James, 10, 61
Hunter, Guy, 8, 11, 56, 116
Hunter, Robert, 10, 61

India, 15, 43, 45, 47, 63, 116
  and tariff quotas, 58, 110
  US aid to, 63
  population, 125
Inter-American Development Bank (IDB), 16
International Bank for Reconstruction and Development (IBRD), (*see* World Bank)
International Development Association (IDA), 24, 31, 42, 77
International Monetary Fund (IMF), 13n, 14, 37
Italy, 27, 44, 98, 110n

Jackson Report, The, 14, 15
Japan, 12, 17, 19
  private investment, 32
  effect of exchange rate changes, 65
  trade, 74, 120
Johnson, Professor H., 122
Joint Dependent Territories Division (DTD), 35–6

King, R. B. M. (*The Planning of the British Aid Programme*), 45n

Least developed countries, 120
Lougheed, A. L. 'The Common Agricultural Policy and International Trade', 105n

McNamara, Robert, 8n, 16, 117
Mansholt Plan, The, 103
Martin, Edwin (*Development Assistance*), 8
Minhas, B. S. (*Mass Poverty and Strategy of Rural Development in India*), 116n
Ministry of Overseas Development (ODM), 34, 35, 36

Netherlands
  aid programme, 11, 77
  aid contribution, 11n, 31, 80–5
    terms, 83, 89
    target commitment, 25
  aid policy, 78–80, 84, 88–91
  geographical distribution of aid, 82–3, 98
  untying of funds, 83–4
  aid management, 85
  private investment, 87–88, 89
Neville Rolfe, E. (*Food, Farming and the Common Market*), 104n
Nixon, President, New Economic Policy (NEP), 10, 12, 61, 65, 68, **75**
Norway, 17, 25, 31, 32

Organisation for European Co-operation and Development (OECD), 8, 37, 54, 77
Overseas Aid, Select Committee on, 34–8, 40, 42, 44–7, 51
Overseas Development Administration (ODA), 35–6, 37, 38, 41, 42, 45, 46, 48
  private investment department of, 48n
  Conference 1970, 116
Overseas Development Council (ODC), 10, 61n

Pajestka, Professor Joseph, ('The Social Dimensions of Development'), 121n, 122, 123, 125

Overseas Development Institute

The Overseas Development Institute (ODI) is an independent, non-government body aiming to promote wise action in the field of overseas development. It was set up in 1960 and is financed by donations from British business and by grants from American foundations and other sources. Its policies are determined by its Council.

The functions of the Institute are :

1   to provide a centre for research in development issues and problems, and to conduct studies of its own;

2   to be a forum for the exchange of views and information among those, in Britain and abroad, who are directly concerned with overseas development in business, in government, and in other organisations;

3   to keep the urgency of development issues and problems before the public and the responsible authorities.